self-
DETERMINATION

self-
DETERMINATION

Instructional and Assessment Strategies

MICHAEL L. WEHMEYER ◆ SHARON L. FIELD

CORWIN PRESS
A SAGE Publications Company
Thousand Oaks, CA 91320

For information:

 Corwin Press
A Sage Publications Company
2455 Teller Road
Thousand Oaks, California 91320
www.corwinpress.com

Sage Publications Ltd.
1 Oliver's Yard
55 City Road
London EC1Y 1SP
United Kingdom

Sage Publications India Pvt. Ltd.
B-42, Panchsheel Enclave
Post Box 4109
New Delhi 110 017 India

Printed in the United States of America.

Library of Congress Cataloging-in-Publication Data

Wehmeyer, Michael L.
Self-determination: Instructional and assessment strategies / Michael L. Wehmeyer,
Sharon L. Field.
    p. cm.
Includes bibliographical references and index.
ISBN-1-4129-2573-8 or 13: 978-1-4129-2573-0 (cloth : alk. paper)
ISBN-1-4129-2574-6 or 13: 978-1-4129-2574-7 (pbk. : alk. paper)
    1. Children with disabilities—Education. 2. Autonomy (Psychology)
3. Choice (Psychology) I. Field, Sharon L. II. Title.

LC4019.W43 2007
371.9′043—dc22   2006025910

07   08   09   10   11   10   9   8   7   6   5   4   3   2   1

Acquisitions Editor:	Kathleen McLane
Editorial Assistant:	Jordan Barbakow
Production Editor:	Diane S. Foster
Copy Editor:	Colleen B. Brennan
Typesetter:	C&M Digitals (P) Ltd.
Proofreader:	Cheryl Rivard
Indexer:	Will Ragsdale
Cover Designer:	Scott Van Atta

Contents

Preface

Promoting the self-determination of students with disabilities has become best practice in the field of special education since it became a focus of interest in special education research and practice in the late 1980s. This initiative was stimulated with funding from the U.S. Department of Education's Office of Special Education Programs (OSEP) to support model projects that identified the skills and characteristics necessary for students with disabilities to become more self-determined, as well as identifying the in-school and out-of-school experiences that lead to the development of self-determination. Due largely to the federal emphasis on and funding to promote self-determination as a component of the education of youth with disabilities, there are now empirically based methods, programs, and strategies to support instruction to achieve this outcome. Further, there are now several empirical studies that demonstrate that enhanced self-determination improves the educational outcomes of youth with disabilities. As such, it is important that teachers be aware of the importance of promoting self-determination and be able to access and use proven methods, materials, and strategies to promote this outcome.

This text is intended to be a user-friendly guide to instructional and assessment strategies that enable teachers to promote student self-determination. While the content is theory driven and based on sound research, the text's focus is on instructional and assessment strategies that enable teachers to promote the self-determination of children and youth with disabilities. Moreover, we place these instructional and assessment strategies in the context of inclusive educational practices and standards-based reform and access to the general curriculum. The primary audience for the text is educators working with students with disabilities (across all categorical areas), as well as school administrators and higher education students preparing to work with students with disabilities.

ACKNOWLEDGMENTS

The authors would like to acknowledge the patience and support of Kathleen McLane at Corwin Press. In addition, we would like to acknowledge the contribution to this text made by our friends and colleagues who have been involved in efforts to promote and enhance self-determination. Dr. Michael Ward was bureau chief for the OSEP Secondary Education and Transition Services, and as well as being a good friend and colleague to both of us, he deserves the credit for being, as it were, the "father of the self-determination movement" in special education. The work of other colleagues, including Laurie Powers, James E. Martin, Laura Huber Marshall, Martin Agran, Carolyn Hughes, Chris Mason, Bonnie Doren, Andy Halpern, Ann Fullerton, Deanna Sands, Colleen Thoma, David Test, Wendy Wood, Michael West, Dalun Zhang, Brian Abery, Dennis Mithaug, Roger Stancliffe, Diane Bassett, Jean Lehmann, Loretta Serna, and others we've likely missed (our apologies), has informed our work and influenced this text.

Sharon Field would like to acknowledge Alan Hoffman, Shlomo Sawilowsky, and Kay Cornell, self-determination research colleagues and coauthors at Wayne State University (WSU); the Self-Determined Educator National Review Panel (Paula Kohler, Deanna Sands, Mike Ward, Ann Fullerton, Juliana Taymans, Mary Morningstar, and Ann Turnbull); and WSU College of Education Dean Paula Wood and Associate Dean for Research Steven Ilmer, who have provided enduring support for self-determination research initiatives at WSU.

Michael Wehmeyer would like to acknowledge the efforts of colleagues at the University of Kansas Beach Center on Disability and Kansas University Center on Developmental Disabilities, including Ann and Rud Turnbull, Susan Palmer, Jane Soukup, Jennifer Lattimore, and Wendy Parent, as well as colleagues in the Kansas University Department of Special Education.

Corwin Press gratefully acknowledges the contributions of the following reviewers:

Erik Carter
Assistant Professor
Department of Rehabilitation Psychology and Special Education
University of Wisconsin-Madison
Madison, Wisconsin

Sally Coghlan, MEd, NBCT
Special Education Department Chair
Rio Linda Junior High School
Rio Linda, California

Marianne Mooney, PhD
Senior Research Associate
TransCen, Inc.
Rockville, Maryland

Marianne Moore
Instructional Specialist
Virginia Department of Education
Richmond, Virginia

Melinda R. Pierson, PhD
Professor
Department of Special Education
California State University, Fullerton
Fullerton, California

About the Authors

 **Michael L. Wehmeyer,** PhD, is Professor of Special Education; Director, Kansas University Center on Developmental Disabilities; and Associate Director, Beach Center on Disability, all at the University of Kansas. Dr. Wehmeyer is engaged in teacher personnel preparation in the area of severe, multiple disabilities and directs multiple federally funded projects conducting research and model development in the education of students with intellectual and developmental disabilities. He is the author of more than 180 articles or book chapters and has authored, coauthored, or coedited 19 books on disability and education-related issues, including issues pertaining to self-determination, transition, universal design for learning and access to the general curriculum for students with significant disabilities, and technology use by people with cognitive disabilities. He is a Fellow and Board Member of the American Association on Mental Retardation, a past President of the Council for Exceptional Children's Division on Career Development and Transition, and is Editor in Chief for the journal *Remedial and Special Education.* In 1999 Dr. Wehmeyer was the inaugural recipient of the Distinguished Early Career Research Award from the Council for Exceptional Children's Division for Research. In May 2003 he was awarded the American Association on Mental Retardation's National Education Award. Dr. Wehmeyer holds undergraduate and master's degrees in special education from the University of Tulsa and a master's degree in experimental psychology from the University of Sussex in Brighton, England, where he was a Rotary International Teacher of the Handicapped Fellow. He earned his PhD in Human Development and Communication Sciences from the University of Texas at Dallas.

 **Sharon L. Field,** EdD, is Professor (Research) and Codirector of the Center for Self-Determination and Transition in the College of Education at Wayne State University. Her areas of specialization include self-determination, transition and life skills, and applied positive psychological practices. She has directed several federally funded transition and self-determination projects. Through these projects, she developed, with Dr. Alan Hoffman, a model of self-determination and the *Steps to Self-Determination* curriculum and, with Drs. Alan Hoffman and Shlomo Sawilowsky, a self-determination assessment battery. She has written extensively on self-determination for persons with and without disabilities. Her work has included development of materials and strategies to promote self-determination at the early childhood, elementary, secondary, and postsecondary levels. She is also the lead author of *The Self-Determined Educator,* a set of instructional modules for use in initial preparation and staff development settings designed to promote self-determination for teachers, and *Self-Determined Parenting,* an instructional support program for parents. She has direct service experience in schools as a special education teacher, job placement specialist, and administrator. Dr. Field earned her master's degree in special education from the University of Wisconsin–Whitewater and her EdD in educational policy, governance, and administration from the University of Washington.

Self-Determination

What Is It and Why Is It Important to Students With Disabilities?

T he purpose of this book is to provide educators a user-friendly guide to instructional and assessment strategies that enable teachers to promote the self-determination of children and youth with (and without) disabilities. We approach this task with several assumptions that need to be clear from the onset. First, we believe that issues pertaining to self-determination are important for all students, not only for students with disabilities. Thus, to the extent practicable, this book addresses methods, materials, and strategies that can promote the self-determination of all students, not excluding students with disabilities. We would also empha-size that when we refer to "students with disabilities," we mean students across all Individuals With Disabilities Education Act (IDEA) categorical areas, including students with more severe disabilities. Quite simply, we believe that promoting self-determination is a critical instructional objec-tive for all students, and although the focus of this text is primarily on instruction for students receiving special education services, the context in which special educators must necessarily operate today necessitates that the topic not be approached from a disability-only perspective.

This brings up several related assumptions. One is that although issues of self-determination have historically been a focus for secondary educators and transition services, we believe that an instructional focus across the life span is critical for student success. Thus, again to the degree practicable, we identify instructional strategies that are important across elementary, middle/junior, and high school years. Also related to the assumption that instruction to promote self-determination is important for all students is our belief that such instruction should be provided in the context of the general education classroom and linked to the general education curriculum. While there are some specialized strategies to promote self-determination linked to special education–specific practices, primarily to the Individualized Education Program (IEP) planning process, our intent is to identify instructional and assessment activities that can be implemented with students in the general education classroom and linked to the general education curriculum.

This latter focus, instruction linked to the general education curriculum, has been motivated by policy initiatives in the past few years that mandate that the educational programs of all students receiving special education services be driven by the general education curriculum as well as unique student learning needs. As we discuss in Chapter 2, it is a relatively simple task to tie instruction to promote self-determination to the general education curriculum. In so doing, teachers provide students with disabilities the opportunity to learn new skills that will enable them to progress in the general education curriculum and enhance their self-determination.

We begin, though, with an overview of, and introduction to, the self-determination construct and its application and importance to the education of students with disabilities.

SELF-DETERMINATION: WHAT IS IT?

In 1990, when we began our work in the area of self-determination and students with disabilities, there was virtually nothing from special education research or practice that answered the question "What is self-determination?" or addressed its importance for students with disabilities or provided direction for instruction. The following models define and describe self-determination.

A Functional Model of Self-Determination

In 1992, Wehmeyer proposed a definition of self-determined behavior in which such behavior referred to "the attitudes and abilities required to act as the primary causal agent in one's life and to make choices regarding one's actions free from undue external influence or interference" (p. 305). At the heart of that definition was the notion of *causal agency*. The adjective *causal* is defined as expressing or indicating cause; showing the interaction of cause and effect. The term *agent* is a noun that means one who acts or has the authority to act or, alternatively, a force or substance that causes change. Self-determined people are causal agents in their lives. They act with authority to make or cause something to happen in their lives. Causal agency implies more than just causing action, however; it implies that the individual who makes or causes things to happen in his or her life does so with an eye toward causing an effect to accomplish a specific end or to cause or create change; in other words, the individual acts volitionally and intentionally. As opposed to implying strictly that an individual simply causes some event to happen, causal agency implies that action is purposeful or performed to achieve an end.

In 1996, Wehmeyer refined this definition to reflect the types of self-determined behavior. It is common for conversations about self-determination to degrade into queries whether "choosing" to park in one parking spot versus another or other seemingly inconsequential actions are expressions of self-determination. There is an equal tendency to equate self-determination only with the most consequential of decisions, such as marriage, divorce, home buying, and so forth. Neither extreme is, in our estimation, accurate. What was missing from the original definition was that, small or large, self-determined actions contribute to one's quality of life. Thus, in 1996, Wehmeyer refined the definition to include this attribute, suggesting that self-determined behavior is "acting as the primary causal agent in one's life and making choices and decisions *regarding one's quality of life* [italics added] free from undue external influence or interference" (p. 24).

Wehmeyer (2006) further refined the definition, proposing that "self-determined behavior refers to volitional actions that enable one to act as the primary causal agent in one's life and to maintain or improve one's quality of life" (p. 117).

These are definitions of the term *self-determined behavior,* and, as such, it is important to identify what is meant by this class of behavior. Self-determined behavior refers to actions that are identified by four essential characteristics: (1) The person acted autonomously; (2) the behavior(s) are self-regulated; (3) the person initiated and responded to the event(s) in a psychologically empowered manner; and (4) the person acted in a self-realizing manner. These four essential characteristics describe the function of the behavior that makes it self-determined or not. People who consistently engage in self-determined behaviors can be described as self-determined, where the word *self-determined* refers to a dispositional characteristic. Dispositional characteristics involve the organization of cognitive, psychological, and physiological elements in such a manner that an individual's behavior in different situations will be similar (though not identical). Eder (1990) described dispositional states as frequent, enduring tendencies that are used to characterize people and are used to describe important differences between people. As such, people can be described as self-determined based on the functional characteristics of their actions or behaviors. This functional model is depicted graphically in Figure 1.1.

Figure 1.1   Wehmeyer's Functional Model of Self-Determination

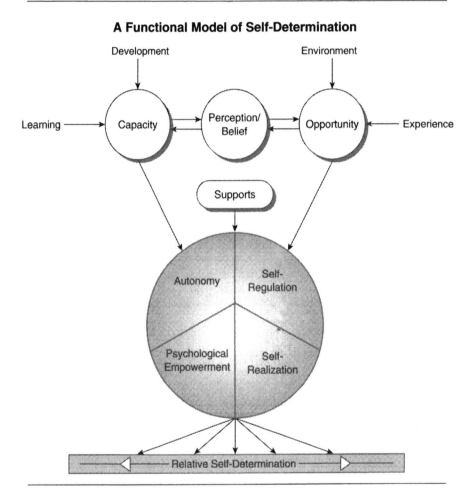

A Functional Model of Self-Determination

Development

Environment

Learning → Capacity ⇄ Perception/Belief ⇄ Opportunity ← Experience

Supports

Autonomy   Self-Regulation

Psychological Empowerment   Self-Realization

← Relative Self-Determination →

Essential characteristics of self-determined behavior. People who are self-determined act autonomously, self-regulate their behavior, and are psychologically empowered and self-realizing. The term *essential characteristic* implies that an individual's actions must reflect, to some degree, each of these four functional characteristics. Age, opportunity, capacity, and circumstances may impact the degree to which any of the essential characteristics are present, and as such, the relative self-determination expressed by an individual will likely vary, sometimes over time and other times across environments. Nonetheless, these essential elements need to be present—each characteristic is a necessary but not sufficient characteristic of self-determined behavior.

Wehmeyer (1999) provided a detailed examination of this theoretical model, but briefly, behavior is *autonomous* if the person acts (a) according to his or her own preferences, interests, and/or abilities; and (b) independently, free from undue external influence or interference. The degree to which people are autonomous reflects the interdependence of all family members, friends, and other people with whom they interact daily as well as the influences of environment and history.

Self-regulation "enables individuals to examine their environments and their repertoires of responses for coping with those environments to make decisions about how to act, to act, to evaluate the desirability of the outcomes of the action, and to revise their plans as necessary" (Whitman, 1990, p. 373). Self-regulated people make decisions about what skills to use in a situation, examine the task at hand and their available repertoire, and formulate, enact, and evaluate a plan of action, with revisions when necessary.

Psychological empowerment consists of the various dimensions of perceived control (Zimmerman, 1990). This includes the cognitive (personal efficacy), personality (locus of control), and motivational domains of perceived control. People who are self-determined are psychologically empowered based on the beliefs that (a) they have the capacity to perform behaviors needed to influence outcomes in their environment, and (b) if they perform such behaviors, anticipated outcomes will result. Finally, self-determined people are *self-realizing* in that they use a comprehensive, and reasonably accurate, knowledge of themselves and their strengths and limitations to act in such a manner as to capitalize on this knowledge in a beneficial way. Self-knowledge forms through experience with, and interpretation of, one's environment and is influenced by evaluations of others, reinforcements, and attributions of one's own behavior.

Self-determination and quality of life. Wehmeyer framed causal agency, and self-determination, within the concept of quality of life. Quality of life is a complex construct that has gained increasing importance as a principle in human services. Schalock (1996) suggested that quality of life is best viewed as an organizing concept to guide policy and practice to improve the life conditions of all people and proposed that quality of life is composed of a number of core principles and dimensions. The eight core principles forwarded by Schalock emphasize that quality of life is composed of the same factors and is important for all people (independent of disability status), is experienced when a person's basic needs are met, and is enhanced by integration and by enabling individuals to participate in decisions that impact their lives. The core dimensions of quality of life include emotional well-being, interpersonal relations, material well-being, personal development, physical well-being, self-determination, social inclusion, and rights.

Component elements of self-determined behavior. Self-determination emerges across the life span as children and adolescents learn skills and develop attitudes that enable them to become causal agents in their own lives. These attitudes and abilities are the component elements of self-determination, and it is this level of the theoretical framework that drives instructional activities. Table 1.1 depicts these component elements.

Table 1.1   Component Elements of Self-Determined Behavior

Choice-Making Skills
Decision-Making Skills
Problem-Solving Skills
Goal-Setting and Attainment Skills
Self-Regulation/Self-Management Skills
Self-Advocacy and Leadership Skills
Positive Perceptions of Control, Efficacy, and Outcome Expectations
Self-Awareness
Self-Knowledge

Because many of the interventions proposed in this book address these component elements, we will not go into any depth on these elements at this point. However, describing the component elements is important for two reasons. First, instruction occurs at this level. That is, there are instructional strategies, methods, materials, and supports that enable educators to "teach" self-determination by enhancing student capacity in each of these areas, as described in subsequent chapters.

Second, each of these component elements has a unique developmental course or is acquired through specific learning experiences, and it is by describing the development of each of these component elements that we can describe the development of self-determination (Doll, Sands, Wehmeyer, & Palmer, 1996; Wehmeyer, Sands, Doll, & Palmer, 1997). The development and acquisition of these component elements is lifelong and begins when children are very young. Some elements have greater applicability for secondary education and transition, while others will focus more on elementary years. As such, promoting self-determination as an educational outcome will require not only a purposeful instructional program but also one that coordinates learning experiences across the span of a student's educational experience.

A Five-Step Model of Self-Determination

Over a three-year research effort, Field and Hoffman (1994) modified a process described by Gordon (1977) to develop a model of self-determination. That process included the following steps: (a) reviewing the literature, (b) conducting interviews, (c) observing students in a variety of school settings, (d) considering internal expertise, and (e) considering external expertise. The model-development process included over 1,500 student observations and interviews with more than 200 individuals. The model was reviewed by panels of experts (including consumers, parents, educators, and adult service providers) in three states and was revised based on their input. In addition, a national review panel of experts provided input on the model and oversaw the model-development process.

Later, the model was revised to clarify and emphasize key elements of self-determination. The revised model (Hoffman & Field, 2006) highlights the importance of these contributing factors to self-determination:

- Understanding of the environment in which one is trying to express self-determination
- The ability to establish and maintain positive relationships
- Skill in focusing on goal(s) the individual has set

Hoffman and Field's (2006) model is depicted in Figure 1.2. As described in this model, self-determination is either promoted or discouraged by factors within the individual's control (e.g., values, knowledge, skills) and variables that are environmental in nature (e.g., opportunities for choice making, attitudes of others).

The model addresses both internal, affective factors and skill components that promote self-determination. The model has five major components: Know Yourself and Your Environment, Value Yourself, Plan, Act, and Experience Outcomes and Learn. The first two components describe internal processes that provide a foundation for acting in a self-determined manner. The next two components, Plan and Act, identify skills needed to act on this foundation. One must have internal awareness as well as the

Figure 1.2 Five-Step Model of Self-Determination

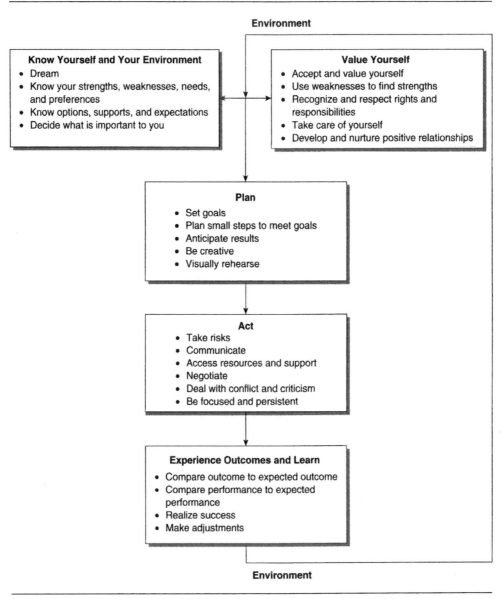

Environment

Know Yourself and Your Environment
- Dream
- Know your strengths, weaknesses, needs, and preferences
- Know options, supports, and expectations
- Decide what is important to you

Value Yourself
- Accept and value yourself
- Use weaknesses to find strengths
- Recognize and respect rights and responsibilities
- Take care of yourself
- Develop and nurture positive relationships

Plan
- Set goals
- Plan small steps to meet goals
- Anticipate results
- Be creative
- Visually rehearse

Act
- Take risks
- Communicate
- Access resources and support
- Negotiate
- Deal with conflict and criticism
- Be focused and persistent

Experience Outcomes and Learn
- Compare outcome to expected outcome
- Compare performance to expected performance
- Realize success
- Make adjustments

Environment

SOURCE: Hoffman, A., & Field, S. (2006). *Steps to self-determination* (2nd ed.). Austin, TX: PRO-ED.

strength and ability to act on that internal foundation to be self-determined. To have the foundation of self-awareness and self-esteem but not the skills, or the skills but not the inner knowledge and belief in the self, is insufficient to fully experience self-determination. To be self-determined, one must know and value what one wants and possess the necessary skills to seek what is desired. The final component in the self-determination model is

Experience Outcomes and Learn. This component includes both celebrating successes and reviewing efforts to become self-determined so that skills and knowledge that contribute to self-determination are enhanced.

Environmental indicators. As stated above, self-determination is affected by environmental variables as well as by the knowledge, skills, and beliefs expressed by the individual. Field and Hoffman (2001) identified nine indicators of environments that support the expression of self-determination.

1. Knowledge, skills, and attitudes for self-determination are addressed in the curriculum, in family support programs, and in staff development.

2. Students, parents, and staff are involved participants in individualized educational decision making and planning.

3. Students, families, faculty, and staff are provided with opportunities for choice.

4. Students, families, faculty, and staff are encouraged to take appropriate risks.

5. Supportive relationships are encouraged.

6. Accommodations and supports for individual needs are provided.

7. Students, families, and staff have the opportunity to express themselves and be understood.

8. Consequences for actions are predictable.

9. Self-determination is modeled throughout the school environment.

SELF-DETERMINATION: WHY IS IT IMPORTANT TO STUDENTS WITH DISABILITIES?

We have defined the self-determination construct and provided two theoretical frameworks constructed within efforts to apply the self-determination construct to the education of students with disabilities. In the next chapter, we overview issues pertaining to the promotion of self-determination in the context of standards-based reform and the general education curriculum. Before doing so, however, we believe it is important to answer the "so what" question. That is, does promoting self-determination matter? Is promoting self-determination important to students with disabilities?

Impact of Promoting Component Elements of Self-Determined Behavior

We begin with evidence that promoting the component elements, identified in Table 1.1, benefits students. A comprehensive review of the impact of component elements of self-determined behavior on adult outcomes is beyond the scope of this chapter, but a brief overview should adequately make the point that there is abundant evidence that promoting the component elements listed in Table 1.1 can result in more positive adult and transition outcomes, including improved employment, community living, and community integration outcomes for students with disabilities.

For example, providing opportunities for and enhancing the capacity of youth and young adults with disabilities to express preferences and make choices have been linked to multiple outcomes of benefit to transition. There is an emerging database showing that incorporating choice-making opportunities into interventions to reduce problem behaviors of children and youth with disabilities results in improved behavioral outcomes (Shogren, Faggella-Luby, Bae, & Wehmeyer, 2004). Research has generally found that when students with autism are provided opportunities to make choices, reductions in problem behavior and increases in adaptive behaviors are observed (Frea, Arnold, & Vittimberga, 2001; Reinhartsen, Garfinkle, & Wolery, 2002).

Cooper and Browder (1998) found that teaching young adults to make choices improved outcomes of community-based instruction. Watanabe and Sturmey (2003) found that promoting choice-making opportunities in vocational tasks for young adults with disabilities increased engagement in the activities.

Teaching effective decision-making and problem-solving skills also has been shown to enhance positive school and transition outcomes for youth and young adults. Teaching young women with intellectual disabilities to make more effective decisions improved their capacity to identify potentially abusive social interactions (Khemka, 2000). Datillo and Hoge (1999) found that teaching decision making, in the context of a leisure education program, to adolescents with cognitive disabilities improved their acquisition of socially valid leisure knowledge and skills.

Limitations in social problem-solving skills have been linked to difficulties in employment, community, and independent living situations for students with developmental disabilities (Gumpel, Tappe, & Araki, 2000). Wiener (2004) confirmed the importance of problem solving to social integration for students with learning disabilities, and Bauminger (2002) showed that teaching students with high-functioning autism social and interpersonal problem-solving skills led to improved social interactions.

Storey (2002) reviewed the empirical literature pertaining to improving social interactions for workers with disabilities and determined that problem-solving skills contributed to more positive workplace social interactions. O'Reilly, Lancioni, and O'Kane (2000) found that incorporating instruction in problem solving into social skills instruction improved employment outcomes for supported workers with traumatic brain injuries. Finally, several studies (Agran, Blanchard, & Wehmeyer, 2000; Palmer, Wehmeyer, Gibson, & Agran, 2004; Wehmeyer, Palmer, Agran, Mithaug, & Martin, 2000) show that teaching students with severe disabilities a self-regulated problem-solving process enables them to self-direct learning and to achieve educationally relevant goals, including transition-related goals.

Similarly, there is research linking enhanced self-management and self-regulation skills to the attainment of positive outcomes. For example, teaching students self-monitoring strategies has been shown to improve the (a) critical learning skills and classroom involvement skills of students with severe disabilities (Agran et al., 2005; Gilberts, Hughes, Agran, & Wehmeyer, 2001; Hughes et al., 2002); (b) math skills of students with learning disabilities and English language learners (Uberti, Mastopieri, & Scruggs, 2004); (c) reading comprehension of students with learning disabilities (Jitendra, Hoppes, & Zin, 2000); (d) math performance by students with severe emotional disturbances (Levendoski & Cartledge, 2000); and (e) on-task behavior of students with autism (Coyle & Cole, 2004).

Research on these and other component elements of self-determined behavior provide strong, though indirect, evidence that youth who are more self-determined achieve more positive adult outcomes. Further, there is an evidence base pertaining to instructional strategies to promote these component elements. Algozzine, Browder, Karvonen, Test, and Wood (2001) conducted meta-analyses of studies reporting intervention strategies to promote component elements of self-determined behavior. The average effect size (ES) across these studies was 1.38, with a standard deviation of 3.74 and a standard error of 0.37. The ES measurements indicated that most studies reported changes in self-determination-related outcomes reflective of a moderate gain as a result of instructional interventions. The single-subject studies demonstrated stronger effect sizes. According to Algozzine et al. (2001), the median percentage of nonoverlapping data (PND) between the treatment and baseline phases was 95% with a range of 64% to 100% for the studies, indicating that participants acquired skills related to self-determination at a relatively high level.

Impact of Promoting Self-Determination

There are only a few studies that provide direct evidence of the relationship between self-determination and student outcomes. Wehmeyer and

Schwartz (1997) measured the self-determination of 80 students with learning disabilities or mental retardation and then examined adult outcomes one year after high school. Students in the high self-determination group were twice as likely (80%) as youth in the low self-determination group to be employed (40%), and earned, on average, $2.00 an hour more than students in the low self-determination group who were employed. There were no significant differences between groups on level of intelligence or number of vocational courses taken. Wehmeyer and Palmer (2003) conducted a second follow-up study, examining adult status of 94 students with cognitive disabilities one and three years postgraduation. One year after high school, students in the high self-determination group were disproportionately likely to have moved from where they were living during high school, and by the third year, they were still disproportionately likely to live somewhere other than their high school home and were significantly more likely to live independently. For employed students, those scoring higher in self-determination made statistically significant advances in obtaining job benefits, including vacation, sick leave, and health insurance, an outcome not shared by their peers in the low self-determination group.

Sowers and Powers (1995) showed that students with disabilities involved in instruction using the TAKE CHARGE materials (described in Chapter 3) to promote self-determination increased their participation and independence in performing community activities. Finally, Wehmeyer and Schwartz (1998) examined the link between self-determination and quality of life for 50 adults with intellectual disabilities. Controlling for level of intelligence and environmental factors, they found that self-determination predicted group membership based on quality of life scores. That is, people who were highly self-determined experienced a higher quality-of-life; people who lacked self-determination appeared to experience a less positive quality of life.

In summary, there is an expanding base of evidence suggesting that higher self-determination and increased capacity in the component elements of self-determined behavior result in better educational and adult outcomes for youth and young adults with disabilities. Chapter 2 explores issues pertaining to promoting self-determination in the context of standards-based reform efforts.

Self-Determination in the Era of Standards-Based Reform

Chapter 1 provided an overview of the self-determination construct and a brief examination of its importance to educational and adult outcomes for children and youth with disabilities. In the more than 15 years since we initially began our work in self-determination, however, the context in which the education of students with disabilities occurs has changed dramatically. This chapter addresses issues pertaining to addressing self-determination in this educational context.

Specifically, the 1997 amendments to the Individuals With Disabilities Education Act (IDEA) introduced statutory and regulatory language pertaining to ensuring access to the general curriculum for students receiving special education services and required that the Individualized Education Program (IEP) of all students receiving special education services include a statement of (a) how the student's disability affects involvement and progress in the general curriculum, (b) the program modifications or supports for school personnel that will be provided for the child to be involved and progress in the general curriculum, and (c) the special education and supplementary aids and services to be provided to ensure a student's involvement in and progress in the general curriculum. IDEA defines *special education* as "specially designed instruction" [20 U.S.C. 1401, SEC. 602, Page 118 Stat. 2657 (29)] and *supplementary aids and services* as "aids, services, and other supports that are provided in regular [general] education classes or other education related settings to enable children with disabilities to be educated with nondisabled children to the maximum extent appropriate" [20 U.S.C. 1401, SEC. 602, Page 118 Stat. 2658 (33)]. The intent of these mandates was to align practice in special education with school reform efforts in general education, efforts that have been codified in the No Child Left Behind Act of 2001 (NCLB).

The 2004 amendments to IDEA continued these 1997 IDEA requirements and extended them, mandating that schools ensure that the IEP team includes someone knowledgeable about the general education curriculum and that it meets at least annually to address any lack of expected progress in the general education curriculum. Finally, the regulations to IDEA 2004 (issued in August 2006) prohibit a student with a disability from being removed from the general education setting based solely on needed modifications to the general education curriculum. The general education curriculum is defined as the same curriculum as provided to students without disabilities and, in practice, is defined by the academic content and student performance standards in each state mandated by NCLB. It is evident, thus, that promoting student access to, and progress in, the general education curriculum remains a focal point of federal policy and national school reform efforts impacting students with disabilities.

These "access to the general education curriculum" requirements were implemented to ensure that students with disabilities were included in emerging standards-based reform and accountability systems. Standards-based reform efforts involve the establishment of state and local content and student achievement standards, in which content standards describe the knowledge, skills, and understanding that students should accomplish in specific content domains, and student achievement standards define the levels of achievement that exemplify proficiency, typically sequenced by grade or age. The curriculum is then developed to align with these standards, and, in turn, teachers are prepared and supported to implement high-quality instructional methods, materials, and strategies to implement the curriculum. Finally, the establishment of high standards, the development of curriculum, and the implementation of high-quality instructional strategies are linked to multiple levels of accountability. That is, the content and student achievement standards are used as measurement criteria to evaluate student progress toward those standards through state and district assessments of student performance.

The IDEA access to the general education curriculum mandates were explicitly intended to ensure that students with disabilities were not excluded from the accountability systems linked with standards-based reform, and NCLB is explicit in its intent that all students will achieve to the same high-quality content standards. It is this alignment with standards-based reform and accountability mechanisms that constitutes the most dramatic element of the changing context in which the education of students with disabilities occurs. While the self-determination initiative was introduced within the context of efforts by the Office of Special Education Programs (OSEP) to promote transition services and influence outcomes for students with disabilities, the access to the general curriculum initiative was introduced within the context of efforts to align special education practices with prevailing reform efforts and, largely, to impact student performance in core content areas. This emphasis on core content areas has been amplified by the steady implementation of assessment-based accountability mechanisms aligned to state and local standards. This is accompanied by an increased emphasis on the importance of evidence-based practices to improve instruction in core content areas such as reading and math.

The concern articulated by policy leaders has been that if students with disabilities are not included in standards-based reform efforts, they will be excluded from the accountability system on which school improvement efforts are based and thus will be marginalized and excluded from efforts to improve academic performance. The same concern might be voiced for educational content areas that are perceived as "outside" of the domain of standards-based reform and accountability, however, including much transition-related instruction such as promoting self-determination (Kochhar-Bryant & Bassett, 2003). While efforts pertaining to promoting access to the general curriculum do not intend to de-emphasize the importance of functional and outcomes-oriented instructional experiences for youth with disabilities, the fact is that the standards-based reform and accountability systems are designed to place increased emphasis on content areas included in standards and tested on assessments linked to those standards. As educators and school districts are increasingly held accountable for outcomes related to district or state assessments, they will increasingly narrow the curriculum to those content areas for which accountability mechanisms are developed and implemented, including, potentially, the focus on self-determination.

Despite these concerns, however, we would suggest that the current context of promoting access to the general education curriculum provides the chance to more fully infuse efforts to promote self-determination into the general education curriculum and that self-determination and student involvement actually provide a means to promote the participation of students with disabilities in the general curriculum. Two ways in which promoting self-determination provides access to and promotes progress in the general education curriculum are described next.

PROMOTING SELF-DETERMINATION IN THE GENERAL EDUCATION CURRICULUM

Self-Determination Content in General Education Standards

State and local standards frequently include goals and objectives that pertain to component elements of self-determined behavior. For example, in virtually every set of state-adopted standards, students are expected to learn and apply effective problem-solving, decision-making, and goal-setting processes and skills. By identifying where in the general curriculum all students are expected to learn skills and knowledge related to the component elements of self-determined behavior, teachers can promote self-determination and promote progress in the general curriculum.

Table 2.1 illustrates some state standards related to promoting self-determination. We searched the standards for five randomly selected states and found content standards, student performance standards, or both across elementary, middle/junior, and high school and across multiple content areas (reading and language arts, science, health education, social studies) that had a specific focus on a component element of self-determined behavior (choice making, problem solving, decision making, goal setting). Keep in mind that these are content and student performance standards that all students in the district are expected to master. If you examine the state and/or local standards in your state or district, we're certain that you will be able to find standards that enable teachers to promote component elements of self-determined behavior.

Self-Determination and Curriculum Modifications

Second, in addition to addressing the component elements of self-determined behavior when they occur in the general education curriculum, teaching young people with and without disabilities skills in self-regulation, self-management, problem solving, goal setting, and decision making enables students to more effectively engage with, and progress through, activities in the general education curriculum. Several models exist to define efforts to promote access to the general curriculum for students with disabilities (Janney & Snell, 2000; Nolet & McLaughlin, 2000). A model proposed by Wehmeyer, Sands, Knowlton, and Kozleski (2002) places particular emphasis on the role of self-determination in two levels of curriculum modifications to enable students to engage with, and respond to, the curriculum.

The first level of modification involves curriculum adaptations. Curriculum adaptation refers to any effort to modify the representation or presentation of the curriculum or to modify the student's engagement with

Table 2.1 State Standards and Self-Determination Content

State	Content Area	Grade	Content Standard	Student Performance Standard
Florida	Language Arts: Reading	6–8	The student constructs meaning from a wide range of texts.	Locate, organize, and interpret written information for a variety of purposes, including classroom research, collaborative decision making, and performing a school or real-world task.
Texas	English Language Arts and Reading	4–8	The student writes for a variety of audiences and purposes and in a variety of forms.	Write to express, discover, record, develop, reflect on ideas, and to problem solve.
New York	Social Studies	K–6	Students will use a variety of intellectual skills to demonstrate their understanding of how the United States and other societies develop economic systems and associated institutions to allocate scarce resources, how major decision-making units function in the United States and other national economies, and how an economy solves the scarcity problem through market and nonmarket mechanisms.	Know that scarcity requires individuals to make choices and that these choices involve costs.
Wisconsin	Health Education	9–12	Students in Wisconsin will demonstrate the ability to use goal-setting and decision-making skills to enhance health.	Demonstrate the ability to use various decision-making strategies related to health needs and risks.
Indiana	Science	7	Students further their scientific understanding of the natural world through investigations, experiences, and readings. They design solutions to practical problems by using a variety of scientific methodologies.	Explain how engineers, architects, and others who engage in design and technology use scientific knowledge to solve practical problems.

the curriculum to enhance access and progress (Rose & Meyer, 2002). Adaptations to the way curricular content is represented refer to the way in which the information in the curriculum is depicted or portrayed, specifically how curricular materials are used to depict information. The dominant representation mode is print, usually through texts, workbooks, and worksheets. There are a number of ways to change that representation, ranging from changing font size to using graphics. Adaptations in curriculum presentation modify the way teachers convey or impart information in the curriculum. Such presentation has, historically, been through written formats (chalkboards or overheads) or verbally (lectures). These primary means of presentation have drawbacks for many students who read ineffectively (or do not read at all) or who have difficulty attending to, or understanding, lecture formats. There are a variety of ways of changing the presentation mode, from using video sources to reading (or playing an audiotape of) written materials to Web-based information.

Curriculum adaptations that modify the student's engagement with the curriculum impact the ways students respond to the curriculum. Again, the typical means of student engagement within the curriculum involves written responses or, perhaps less frequently, oral responses or reports. However, students can respond or engage with the curriculum in multiple other ways, including via drawings, photography, music, role plays, animation, or video (Rose & Meyer, 2002). Each of these enables students to express their ideas and demonstrate their knowledge.

The second level of curricular modification to achieve access involves curriculum augmentation (Knowlton, 1998; Wehmeyer, Lattin, & Agran, 2001; Wehmeyer et al., 2002). With curriculum augmentation, the standard curriculum is enhanced with "meta-cognitive or executive processing strategies for acquiring and generalizing the standard curriculum" (Knowlton, 1998, p. 100). Such augmentations do not change the curriculum but rather add to or augment the curriculum with strategies for students to succeed within the curriculum. The most frequently identified curriculum augmentations instruct students in cognitive strategies or learning-to-learn strategies that enable them to perform more effectively with content in the general curriculum, including reading, writing, notetaking, memory, and test-taking strategies. While primarily developed for students with learning disabilities (Deshler, Ellis, & Lenz, 1996), these strategies can be used with a wide array of students.

Promoting self-determination contributes to both levels of curricular modification (adaptation, augmentation) to promote access to the general curriculum. For example, Kame'enui and Simmons (1999) identified one of the six basic design principles of curriculum adaptation to be the use of "conspicuous strategies":

To solve problems, students follow a set of steps or strategies. Many students develop their own strategies, but a considerable amount of time may be required for the student to identify the optimum strategy. For students with disabilities, such an approach is highly problematic because instructional time is a precious commodity and these learners may never figure out an efficient strategy. Learning is most efficient when a teacher can make it conspicuous or explicit. (p. 15)

Kame'enui and Simmons (1999) illustrated both the core role that problem solving plays in learning and the difficulties students with disabilities experience as a function of their nonstrategic approach to content and activities and their difficulty with goal-oriented actions. Students who learn effectively set learning goals and objectives to reach those goals and then use problem-solving and self-regulation skills to tackle the activities to achieve those goals. Promoting self-determination includes efforts to teach problem-solving, goal-setting, and self-regulation or self-management skills. By augmenting the general curriculum to explicitly teach these skills, teachers are not only promoting self-determination but also providing skills students can apply to learning situations. Teaching students self-directed learning strategies serves as an effective curriculum augmentation as well, with skills such as self-monitoring or self-instruction serving as effective strategies that students can, in turn, apply to the learning process.

INFUSING INSTRUCTION INTO THE GENERAL EDUCATION CURRICULUM

In Chapter 3, we overview methods, materials, and strategies to involve students with disabilities in educational planning and decision making as a means to promote self-determination and introduce assessment procedures that can be used to track student progress and make instructional decisions. In Chapters 4 through 6, we examine instructional methods and strategies to promote self-determination. Methods and strategies are effective, however, only if they are implemented in the context of carefully planned instruction. In the remainder of this chapter, we want to overview the scope and sequence of instruction that can be linked to the component elements of self-determined behavior (see Table 1.1), but to do so in the context of infusing instruction on these component elements into day-to-day instructional activities and, specifically, in the context of standards-linked unit and lesson planning.

Planning

Effective instruction is intentional and planned, and effective instruction to promote self-determination is no different. Moore (2005) suggested that teachers should engage in four levels of instructional planning: course and unit planning, and weekly and daily planning, with these levels going from broad (course) to more detailed (daily).

Course or Curriculum Planning

Whether you teach eighth-grade math, third-grade at an elementary school, or high school civics, there are opportunities to infuse instruction to promote self-determination into your course or the curriculum you will cover (in the case of elementary-level teachers responsible for multiple content areas). There are several common tasks that comprise course or curriculum planning that need to consider issues pertaining to promoting self-determination, including goal setting, decisions pertaining to instructional materials, and identifying the scope and sequence for the course or school year. Before all of these classroom-level activities occur, however, it is useful to have a campuswide understanding of where instruction to promote self-determination can be accomplished in the context of the general education curriculum.

As Table 2.1 shows, because opportunities to teach students the knowledge and skills they will need to be more self-determined can occur across grades and content areas, it is important to make sure that there is a broad road map that ensures that instruction across all component elements is being addressed. One means to achieve this is to incorporate content on self-determination in a curriculum map.

Many schools already use a curriculum mapping process to be sure they are teaching all parts of the curriculum framework, performance objectives, and other standards at the appropriate grade or in the appropriate course (Jacobs, 1997). This process involves the collection of information about each teacher's curriculum, including descriptions of the content to be taught during the year, processes and skills emphasized, and student assessments used, using the school calendar as an organizer. Through a variety of review steps involving all school personnel, a curriculum map for the school is developed. By simply adding self-determination as a content area for which teachers report instructional and assessment activities, a school can create a map of where specific content areas related to self-determination, (e.g., problem solving, decision making, goal setting, etc.) are taught and where there are gaps in such instructional opportunities.

Once the scope and sequence of instruction are determined through curriculum mapping, the next step in the course or curriculum planning process is the establishment of goals and objectives for the course or school year. In the climate of standards-based reform, these goals are generally set by state or district content or, more specifically, student achievement standards. Teachers have little control over the establishment of these goals, obviously, but they can do two things that maximize the self-determination focus. First, as illustrated in Table 2.1, many student achievement standards contain a self-determination focus (solve a problem, make a decision, set a goal, choose an action, etc.), and course or curriculum planning can emphasize instruction on not just the content-related intent but also on instruction to enable the student to perform the self-determination-related activity.

Consider the Wisconsin student achievement standard in Table 2.1 that requires students to "demonstrate the ability to use various decision-making strategies related to health needs and risks." Obviously, one focus of instruction to achieve this goal will be teaching students about health needs and risks. A second self-determination instructional focus could, however, be explicit instruction teaching students how to make a decision. It is often the case that students do not receive direct instruction on skills like how to solve problems, set goals, or make decisions, even when educational goals and objectives specify that students must perform these activities in the context of the content area.

Second, if the content or student achievement goals pertaining to the course or curriculum scope and sequence do not readily lend themselves to a self-determination component, you can create additional goals that focus on the types of self-determination outcomes you'd like to achieve during the course or school year. If you're a first-grade teacher, that goal might focus on improving student capacity to choose from among multiple options and to engage in some rudimentary self-evaluation (e.g., a student comparing her work to an example of high-quality work). A middle school teacher might focus more on providing instruction to enable students to learn to identify and solve simple problems, while a high school teacher's goals might be to teach decision-making skills.

Such goals need, necessarily, to be age appropriate, taking into account student development and previously acquired skills. Table 2.2 provides examples of areas of instructional focus to promote self-determination across four age groups (early childhood, early elementary, late elementary, and secondary).

Another important task involved in course or curriculum planning is the determination of instructional materials that provide content information and related student materials. Often core instructional materials are selected by the district, but even then it is often possible for teachers to order other instructional materials. To ensure that these decisions

Table 2.2   Age-Referenced Instructional Activities to Promote Self-Determination

Early Childhood (Ages 2–5)

- Provide opportunities to make structured choices, such as, "Do you want to wear the blue shirt or the red shirt?" Extend choices across food, clothing, activity, and other choices.
- Provide opportunities to generate choices that are both positive and negative, such as, "We have 10 more minutes. What could we do?" and "You spilled your milk. What could you do to clean it up?"
- Provide formative and constructive feedback on the consequences of choices made in the recent past, such as, "When you pushed hard on the pencil, it broke. What might you want to do the next time?" and "When you used an angry voice, I didn't do what you wanted. What could you do differently?"
- Provide opportunities for planning activities that are pending, such as, "You need to choose a dress to wear to the wedding" or "Decide what kind of sandwich you want to take for lunch tomorrow."
- Provide opportunities to self-evaluate task performance by comparing their work to a model. Point out what they've done that's like the model, such as, "Look, you used nice colors too, just like this one" and "Do you see that you both drew the man from the side?"
- Ask directive questions so that the child compares his or her performance to a model, such as, "Are all of your toys in the basket, too?" or "I'll know you're ready for the story when you are sitting on your mat with your legs crossed, your hands on your knees, and your eyes on me."

Early Elementary (Ages 6–8)

- Provide opportunities to choose from among several different strategies for a task, such as, "Will you remember your spelling words better if you write them out, say them to yourself, or test yourself?" or "What is the easiest way for you to figure out what this word means?"
- Ask children to reconsider choices they've made in the recent past, in light of the subsequent consequences of those choices, such as, "This morning you decided to spend your lunch money on the comic. Now it's lunchtime and you're hungry. What decision do you wish you'd made?" or "I remember when you decided to leave your coat in your locker. What happened because you made that decision?"
- Encourage children to "think aloud" with you, saying the steps that they are taking to complete a task or solve a problem, such as, "Tell me what you're thinking in your head while you try to figure out what the word means" or "You've lost your house key. What are you thinking to yourself while you decide what to do?"
- Provide opportunities for students to talk about how they learn, such as, "Is it easier for you to tell me what you want by saying it or by writing it down?" or "Do you remember better if you study for a test all at once or a little bit on several different days?" Help students test out their answers.
- Provide opportunities for students to systematically evaluate their work, such as, "Here's a very neat paper, and here's your paper. Is your paper as neat as this one? What are the differences between this paper and yours? How are they alike?"

- Help students set simple goals for themselves and check to see whether they are reaching them, such as, "You said you want to read two books this week. How much of a book have you read so far? Let's color in your goal sheet so you can see how much you've done."

Late Elementary (Ages 9–11)

- Provide guidance in systematic analyses of decisions: writing the problem at the top of a sheet of paper, listing all possible choices, and sketching out the benefits and cost of each choice.
- Use the same systematic structure to analyze past decisions now that their consequences are evident, such as, "You were angry at Jo for teasing you, and so you punched her in the cheek. Now you have to sit out at recess for a week. What are some other things that you could have done instead? What might have happened then?"
- Provide opportunities for students to commit to personal or academic goals: writing the goal down and storing it in a safe place, revisiting the goal periodically to reflect on progress toward it, listing optional steps to take toward the goal, and trying out the steps and reflecting on their success.
- Provide opportunities to systematically analyze adult perspectives, such as the point of view of the volleyball coach when a student is late to every game or the perspective of the librarian when a student returns a book that is dirty and torn. Help the student guess what the adult is thinking and feeling and what might be done as a result.
- Provide opportunities for students to evaluate task performance in effectively "safe" ways: identifying weaknesses and strengths in performance, reflecting on ways to improve performance, trying out some ways, and reevaluating performance to check for improvement. For example, "You got a lower grade than you wanted on your research paper. What steps did you take to make it a really strong paper? What steps did you leave out? What might you do now to make it even better?"

Secondary (Ages 12–18)

- Provide opportunities for students to make decisions that have an important impact on their day-to-day activities, such as academic goals, careers to explore, schedules to keep, diet and sleep habits, and others.
- Make it easy for students to see the link between goals they set for themselves and the daily decisions that they make, such as, "You made a point of going to bed early last night, and now I see you earned a 95 on today's quiz. Going to bed on time seems to be helping you meet your goal of higher grades this semester," or "You've set aside half of every paycheck, and now you have $625 in the bank. It won't be long before you have enough to buy the computer you want."
- Provide guidance in breaking students' long-term goals into a number of short-term objectives. Lead students through planning activities to determine steps to take to progress toward these goals. For example, help a student break the goal of a higher math grade into smaller objectives of rechecking math homework before handing it in, practicing the math problems on nights before the test, and asking questions whenever something isn't clear.

(Continued)

Table 2.2 (Continued)

- Assist the student in realistically recognizing and accepting weaknesses in key skills. You might say, for example, "It's hard for you to do your math problems without making mistakes in your math facts. What are some parts of math that you're good at? What could you do to get around the reality that you don't remember math facts well?"
- Assist students in requesting academic and social supports from teachers. Say, for example, "You'd like Mrs. Green to let you have some extra time to complete the weekly quiz. How will you ask her for that?" or "You think you'd do better work if your boss would let you use a note pad to jot down the orders. What can you do to ask for that?"

SOURCE: Doll, B., Sands, D. J., Wehmeyer, M. L., & Palmer, S. (1996). Promoting the development and acquisition of self-determined behavior. In D. J. Sands & M. L. Wehmeyer (Eds.), *Self-determination across the life span: Independence and choice for people with disabilities* (pp. 63–88). Baltimore: Brookes.

contribute to efforts to promote self-determination, you can preview instructional materials and ask the following types of questions:

- Do these materials foster autonomous learning, or are they overly directive in nature?
- Do the materials engage students in problem-solving activities?
- In what ways can students engage with the materials and respond to show their knowledge? Are these unnecessarily static (e.g., only worksheets), or do they provide for multiple means of engagement?
- Do the materials lend themselves to the kind of modifications you will need to make to ensure access for all learners?

This is a good time to bring up the issue of the importance of Universal Design for Learning (UDL), not only to ensure access to content for all students but, additionally, to promote self-determination. Universal Design for Learning (or just UDL) refers to the design of instructional materials to make the content information available to all children. The Council for Exceptional Children defined UDL as "the design of instructional materials and activities that allows the learning goals to be achievable by individuals with wide differences in their abilities to see, hear, speak, move, read, write, understand English, attend, organize, engage, and remember" (Orkwis & McLane, 1998, p. 9).

It is obvious that students who cannot read, who do not speak or read English well, or who have a learning disability affecting their capacity to decode written text will not be able to access academic content if it is presented only in written textbooks. Similarly, students with other health impairments or attention deficit hyperactivity disorder may not be able to acquire content if it is presented solely in lecture format. Universally designed materials are those that, in essence, remove the necessity to adapt the curriculum and build in flexibility in content representation and student engagement from the onset.

Teachers achieve flexibility in representing content representation and presenting it when they use multiple formats, including text, graphics or pictures, digital and other media formats (audio or video, movies), or performance formats (plays, skits), and when they use different means to deliver content information, including lectures, visual presentations (PowerPoint), role playing, or computer-mediated instruction. Similarly, students can provide evidence of their learning through reports or exams, portfolios, drawings or performances, oral reports, videotaped reports, and other alternative means.

When engaged in course and curriculum planning, teachers must choose materials that provide the kind of flexibility ensured by UDL, because unless students have access to content information, they will not be able to learn, and because using multiple, flexible types of instructional materials almost inevitably leads to greater student involvement in, and self-direction of, the learning activities. Compare, for example, technology-mediated instruction (or computer-based instruction) with typical text-book and lecture-based instruction. When content is available to students in digital and electronic formats, it can be presented in ways that maximize multiple representations (audio, video) and, by its very nature, be interactive. Such instruction promotes autonomy and self-determination as well as providing content instruction.

A third major task of course or curriculum planning is the identification of units or themes, the sequence of these units, and the means to evaluate their effectiveness. Unit evaluations resemble program evaluation more than individual student evaluation. In Chapter 7, we talk about ways to perform such evaluations in a manner that promotes self-determination. It is at the course or curriculum planning level, though, that teachers must identify the "big ideas" they want to achieve in each unit. Wiggins and McTighe (1998) talk about these big ideas as planning for enduring understanding.

> Teaching is more than covering content, learning is more than merely taking in, and assessment is more than accurate recall. Meaning must be made, and understanding must be earned. Students are more likely to make meaning and gain understanding

when they link new information to prior knowledge, relate facts to "big ideas," explore essential questions, and apply their learning in new contexts. (McTighe, Seif, & Wiggins, 1998, p. 26)

The big ideas are those concepts, knowledge, and skills that you want all students to attain and, as the notion of enduring understanding suggests, retain. These big ideas form the foundation for later planning activities that use cognitive taxonomies to differentiate unit and lesson goals and instruction, so it is critical that you identify these from the onset. Obviously, if you want instruction to promote self-determination, then you need to plan for enduring understanding in the component elements of self-determined behavior as well as the specific content.

Once big ideas are formulated, course or curriculum planning proceeds with the specification of major topics and concepts (units), their sequence, and how much time will be allotted to each. If you're responsible for teaching a major aspect of self-determined behavior, say, teaching students the basics of solving a problem, it will be important to factor that into the time needed for the unit.

Unit and Lesson Planning

Once unit topics and key concepts are identified, teachers move to the level of unit planning, then to lesson planning. These differ as a function of the depth of planning and the time covered by the plan. Unit plans require a longer period of time to cover, state the educational goals and objectives for the unit, identify methods to be used and resources needed, and determine an overall evaluation framework. Lesson plans can be weekly or daily and provide greater specificity in instructional goals and objectives; they may include specifics about lesson components like an introductory activity, specific strategies to be implemented, means of assessing student progress, and a closing activity (Moore, 2005).

Our intent is not to go into great detail on the unit and lesson planning processes but instead to identify how these processes support instruction to promote self-determination.

Turn, for example, to the Indiana science standards for Grade 7, identified in Table 2.1. The seventh-grade content standard from the Indiana science standards states:

Students further their scientific understanding of the natural world through investigations, experiences, and readings. They design solutions to practical problems by using a variety of scientific methodologies.

Logically, this standard can become one of the primary course or curriculum goals for the year. In addition, this content standard makes it evident that student knowledge about problem solving is a critical content feature of this course. By considering some of the student performance standards that, equally logically, will become unit-level goals, teachers can acquire greater detail about unit and lesson goals to promote self-determination. For example, under the Grade 7 science content standard, there are two student performance standards that relate to problem solving:

- Explain that what people expect to observe often affects what they actually do observe and provide an example of a solution to this problem.
- Explain how engineers, architects, and others who engage in design and technology use scientific knowledge to solve practical problems.

It would be quite simple to teach problem solving using the student performance standards as unit goals. For example, with the second such standard (explain how engineers, architects, and others who engage in design and technology use scientific knowledge to solve practical problems), you might create a lesson plan, such as that in Table 2.3, that explicitly teaches problem-solving skills as an accompaniment to the science lessons themselves.

Another means to ensure that unit and lesson plans are written to focus on self-determination is to incorporate student-directed learning strategies such as self-monitoring, self-instruction, and self-evaluation (all discussed in Chapter 6) into the strategies section of the lesson plan. It is also in the unit and lesson plans that teachers can identify what universally designed materials are used and what curriculum modifications will be needed to ensure access for all students.

Cognitive and learning taxonomies. Before describing specific content information to promote self-determination, it is worth noting that one critical feature of unit and lesson plans that ensures differentiation of instruction is the use of cognitive taxonomies, a practice that is equally important to ensure that all students have an opportunity to acquire knowledge and skills related to self-determination. It is evident that students will vary greatly in the complexity with which they interact with and respond to the content provided. Even if one ensures access to all through UDL materials and curriculum modifications, it is inevitable that students will differ in their capacities and experiences in ways that impact what they will achieve. The purpose of identifying the big ideas is to identify what

Table 2.3   Sample Lesson Plan for Teaching Problem Solving

Unit Goal: Explain how engineers, architects, and others who engage in design and technology use scientific knowledge to solve practical problems.

Lesson Goal: Define a problem and teach basic steps to solving a problem.

Objectives:

Each student will:

1. Define a problem and provide an example across multiple domains.
2. Demonstrate knowledge of five basic steps to problem solving.

Introductory Activity:

Tell the students that each of the following questions tells the beginning of a story and how the story ends. Their job is to tell what happened in the middle of the story, to connect the beginning and the end. Read the beginning of each story and then ask students to identify the best answer they can think of for the middle of the story. Emphasize that there are no right or wrong answers. Read each story beginning and end, and then solicit answers, writing each one down without comment.

1. Beginning: Your book report is due tomorrow, but you just realized that you left the book you need to write the report on at school.

   Ending: The story ends with you turning in your book report the next day.

2. Beginning: You are meeting with your teacher and parents. You want to take a class where you can learn skills to help you work in hotel management. Your parents want you to take the Family and Child Care class. You can take only one of the classes.

   Ending: The story ends with you taking a class where you will learn hotel management.

3. Beginning: You hear a friend talking about a new job opening at the local bookstore. You love books and want a job. You decide you would like to work at the bookstore.

   Ending: The story ends with you working at the bookstore.

4. Beginning: You go to your English class one morning and discover your English book is not in your backpack. You are upset because you need that book to do your homework.

   Ending: The story ends with you using your English book for homework.

As a final introductory activity, tell the students that you have two trees in your front yard. Both trees are the same species, a red maple; both were bought from the same nursery and were planted on the same day; and both were the same size when they were planted. Now, 10 years later, however, one tree is much smaller than the other. Ask the students to give reasons why that might happen.

Content:

I. What is a problem?
   a. Defining problems
   b. Problem domains
      i. Scientific
      ii. Social
      iii. Mathematical
   c. Problem solving as a process

II. Steps to problem solving
   a. Identify the problem.
   b. Define the problem.
   c. Consider alternatives to solve the problem.
   d. Select a preferred solution.
   e. Evaluate the effectiveness of the chosen solution.

Procedure:

1. After the introductory activity, ask students in the class what they have been doing. Support students to identify that each of the scenarios presented a problem that needed to be solved.

2. Ask students how they define *problem*. Your goal is to have students eventually define a problem as simply a situation, task, or activity in which a difficulty exists and the answer to that difficulty is not immediately known or readily apparent. Direct students to shape their responses with the following questions:
   a. Some people think about problems as only bad things. Are all problems bad?
   b. What is at the heart of all problems? (A difficulty or dilemma)
   c. What kinds of problems do you know about?
      i. Math problems
      ii. Puzzles, such as Sudoku
      iii. Science problems
      iv. Personal or social problems (with other people)

3. Explain that solving problems involves a process with five steps.
   a. Ask students to tell what a *process* is. (A series of actions or steps that lead to an outcome or result)
   b. Present the five steps to problem solving:
      i. Identify the problem.
      ii. Define the problem.
      iii. Consider alternatives to solve the problem.
      iv. Select a preferred solution.
      v. Evaluate the effectiveness of the chosen solution.

(Continued)

Table 2.3 (Continued)

---

4. Return to the different-sized tree problem presented in the introductory activity and have students, as a whole group, brainstorm the problem-solving process they could use to solve that problem. In general, look for the outcomes to resemble this:
   a. Identify the problem.
      i. One tree is smaller than the other.
         1. This might indicate the smaller tree is less healthy.
         2. This might indicate a problem with the soil in one part of your yard that may affect other plants and landscaping.

   b. Define the problem.
      i. Once students brainstorm possible problems, have them clearly state what the problem is in specific terms.
         1. Acceptable: One tree is smaller than the other. The two trees are not the same size.
         2. Unacceptable: It's not right. It doesn't look good.

   c. Consider alternatives to solve the problem. (The intent is not to identify the actual problem; it is to generate as many reasonable solutions as possible.)
      i. Soil differences (iron deficiency, poor pH balance)
      ii. Watering differences (draught, overwatering)
      iii. Tree diseases
      iv. Different access to sunlight
      v. Other

   d. Select a preferred solution.
      i. Discuss with students how they might select the correct solution (soil testing, inspecting tree, etc.).

   e. Evaluate the effectiveness of the chosen solution.
      i. Discuss with students the steps they could take to see if their solution was correct.

---

you want every child to learn. However, it is unfair to students in the class to set a lesson objective that is either too simple for some students or too difficult for others. The solution to this is to use cognitive and learning taxonomies to differentiate lesson objectives.

Cognitive taxonomies are used to classify the cognitive demands of learning targets (Biehler & Snowman, 1993). Perhaps the most familiar such taxonomy is the one developed by Bloom and associates (1956). Bloom's taxonomy, depicted in Table 2.4, is a means of categorizing the cognitive skills students use when achieving learning targets. As one ascends Bloom's taxonomy, the cognitive demands from students are more complex.

As cognitive taxonomies are applied in lesson planning activities, teachers track whether they are introducing students to increasingly complex

Table 2.4   Bloom's Taxonomy

Category	Definition	Related Behaviors
Knowledge	Recalling or remembering something without necessarily understanding, using, or changing it.	Define, describe, identify, label, list, match, memorize, point to, recall, select, state.
Comprehension	Understanding something that has been communicated without necessarily relating it to anything else.	Alter, account for, annotate, calculate, change, convert, group, explain, generalize, give examples, infer, interpret, paraphrase, predict, review, summarize, translate.
Application	Using a general concept to solve problems in a particular situation; using learned material in new and concrete situations.	Apply, adopt, collect, construct, demonstrate, discover, illustrate, infer, outline, point out, select, separate, sort, subdivide.
Analysis	Breaking something down into its parts; may focus on identification of parts or analysis of relationships between parts, or recognition of organization principles.	Analyze, compare, contrast, diagram, differentiate, dissect, distinguish, identify, illustrate, infer, outline, point out, select, separate, sort, subdivide.
Synthesis	Creating something new by putting parts of different ideas together to make a whole.	Blend, build, change, combine, compile, compose, conceive, create, design, formulate, generate, hypothesize, plan, predict, produce, reorder, revise, tell, write.
Evaluation	Judging the value of material or methods as they might be applied in a particular situation; judging with the use of definite criteria.	Accept, appraise, assess, arbitrate, award, choose, conclude, criticize, defend, evaluate, grade, judge, prioritize, recommend, referee.

SOURCE: Adapted from Bloom, B., Englehart, M., Furst, E., Hill, W., & Krathwohl, D. (1956). *Taxonomy of educational objectives: The classification of educational goals.* New York: Longmans.

skills and content. When learning objectives are set, students are expected to demonstrate their competence across levels of higher-ordered thinking skills and content types. Once a learning target has been specified, curriculum decision makers also must consider the previous experiences of the learner with a skill or topic. Haring, Liberty, and White (1980) categorized learning into five phases: (1) acquisition, (2) fluency, (3) generalization, (4) adaptation, and (5) maintenance. This learning taxonomy helps teachers to distinguish between those curriculum activities they might use if learners had no prior experience with a task or skill to be learned versus those that might be used to make sure that students continue to maintain their accuracy with a well-learned skill, and it provides the basis for further differentiation.

Curriculum Content

We have suggested that instruction to promote self-determination can be linked to state and local district standards across content areas and grade levels, and that course and curriculum, unit, and lesson planning can take advantage of this and integrate instruction on component elements of self-determined behavior (see Table 1.1) into instruction across content areas. In this section, we briefly identify some critical content and instructional areas that should be considered.

Goal Setting

Goal setting and attainment skills are critical for all students to become more self-determined. Goals specify what a person wishes to achieve and act as regulators of human behavior. If a person sets a goal, it increases the probability that he or she will perform behaviors related to that goal (Latham & Locke, 1991). The process of promoting goal-setting and attainment skills involves teaching students to (a) identify and define a goal clearly and concretely, (b) develop a series of objectives or tasks to achieve the goal, and (c) specify the actions necessary to achieve the desired outcome. At each step, students must make choices and decisions about what goals they wish to pursue and what actions they wish to take to achieve their goals. Goal-setting activities can be easily incorporated into a variety of content-related activities and across multiple instructional areas, as well as in the IEP planning process, as discussed in Chapter 3.

Choice Making

Choice making is simply the expression of a preference between two or more options and is a particularly important component to incorporate into instruction in the early elementary years. By making choices, younger students learn that they can exert control over their environment. For students to fully understand the process of choice making, including the various effects of making certain choices, choices need to be real and meaningful for students. Some students with more severe disabilities may, in fact, need to be taught how to make choices, particularly if their previous opportunities to do so have been restricted. To do this, picture cues can be used to teach students to choose between two or more depicted activities, with the selection of an activity followed immediately by performance of the activity (Bambara & Ager, 1992).

Choice opportunities can and should be infused throughout the school day during the early elementary years for all students. Students can be provided opportunities to choose within or between instructional activities. They can also choose with whom they engage in a task, where they engage in an activity, and if they complete an activity (Brown, Appel, Corsi, & Wenig, 1993).

Problem Solving

As we've already discussed, a problem is an activity or task for which a solution is not known or readily apparent. The process of solving a problem involves (a) identifying and defining the problem, (b) listing possible solutions, (c) identifying the impact of each solution, (d) making a judgment about a preferred solution, and (e) evaluating the efficacy of the judgment (D'Zurilla & Goldfried, 1971; Izzo, Pritz, & Ott, 1990).

Sorenson, Buckmaster, Francis, and Knauf (1996) identified reasons why "all students must be able to solve problems" (p. 2). These included the following:

- Solving problems successfully is crucial to the global workplace.
- Solving problems is personally satisfying.
- Solving problems encourages independent learning.
- Solving problems enhances success in school.
- Solving problems is vital to a democratic society.

We would suggest that these justify infusing problem-solving instruction into the curriculum as well as focusing on self-determination.

Decision Making

A decision-making process involves coming to a judgment about which solution is best at a given time. Making effective decisions typically involves (a) identifying alternative courses of action, (b) identifying the possible consequences of each action, (c) assessing the probability of each consequence occurring, (d) choosing the best alternative, and (e) implementing the decision (Beyth-Marom, Fischhoff, Quadrel, & Furby, 1991;

Furby & Beyth-Marom, 1992). Although the ability to engage in this process develops with age, research has shown that young children can engage in a systematic decision-making process, often by reducing and simplifying the steps in the decision-making process, although they are not as effective as older students (Crone, Vendel, & van der Molen, 2003). Thus, working to promote systematic decision-making skills is best addressed at the secondary level, while at the elementary level, a focus on choice making and problem solving can support the development of effective decision-making skills later in life.

Self-Regulation and Student-Directed Learning

Each of the aforementioned areas—goal setting, choice making, problem solving, and decision making—is important to enable students to self-regulate their behavior and their lives. Self-regulation is the process of setting goals, developing action plans to achieve those goals, implementing and following the action plans, evaluating the outcomes of the action plan, and changing actions plans if the goal was not achieved (Mithaug, 1993; Mithaug, Mithaug, Agran, Martin, & Wehmeyer, 2003). The skills associated with self-regulation enable students to examine their environments, evaluate their repertoire of possible responses, and implement and evaluate a response (Whitman, 1990).

Student-directed learning strategies are those that enable students to modify and regulate their own behavior (Agran, 1997). The emphasis in such strategies is shifted from teacher-mediated and -directed instruction to student-directed instruction. Research in education and rehabilitation has shown that student-directed learning strategies are as successful as, and often more successful than, teacher-directed learning strategies and that these strategies are effective means to increase independence and productivity. A variety of strategies have been used to teach students with disabilities how to manage their own behavior or direct learning, including picture cues and antecedent cue regulation strategies, self-instruction, self-monitoring, self-evaluation, and self-reinforcement (Agran, King-Sears, Wehmeyer, & Copeland, 2003). In Chapter 6, we go into detail on how you can teach students to self-regulate learning through student-directed learning strategies.

Self-Advocacy

All students, but particularly perhaps students with disabilities, need to learn the skills to advocate on their own behalf. To be an effective self-advocate, students have to learn both how to advocate and what to advocate for. There are ample opportunities for students to practice and learn self-advocacy skills within the context of the educational planning process, and we return to this topic and provide more explicit examples of promoting self-advocacy in Chapter 3 when we discuss promoting student involvement in educational planning, but it should be noted that you can infuse instruction to promote self-advocacy in classroom activities as well as in the IEP meeting.

Perceptions of Efficacy and Control

People who have positive perceptions of their efficacy believe they can perform the behavior required to achieve a desired outcome (Bandura, 1977; Bandura & Cervone, 2000). Further, individuals also have efficacy expectations, which are beliefs about the probability of the performance of a given behavior leading to the desired outcome. People who believe they have the ability to exert control over their lives and outcomes tend to be described as having an internal locus of control, whereas people who perceive that others are largely in control of their lives and outcomes are described as having an external locus of control (Rotter, 1954, 1966). Research has shown that students' perceptions of control and efficacy interact with academic, social, and behavioral outcomes, with students who have more adaptive perceptions of their abilities in each of these areas experiencing more positive outcomes (Hagborg, 1996; Wehmeyer, 1994).

Students need to be provided with opportunities to develop adaptive perceptions of their efficacy in performing given behaviors and their ability to exert control over their lives. By enabling students to engage in problem solving and goal setting, and to make choices and decisions that are meaningful, they can learn that they have control over their outcomes and develop confidence in their ability to perform these behaviors and achieve their desired outcomes. Both teacher and classroom characteristics can influence students' perceptions of efficacy and control. Overly controlling environments can diminish students' perceptions of their ability to exert control and engage in actions that enable them to develop adaptive efficacy expectations. It is important for teachers to work to empower students to be active participants in their classrooms.

Self-Awareness and Self-Knowledge

For students to become more self-realizing, they must possess a reasonably accurate understanding of their strengths, abilities, unique learning and support needs, and limitations. Further, they must know how to utilize this understanding to maximize success and progress. However, like perceptions of efficacy and control, self-awareness and knowledge are not something that can simply be taught through direct instruction.

Instead, students acquire this knowledge by interacting with their environment. Unfortunately, students with disabilities often learn to identify what they *cannot* do instead of what they can. This skews students' perceptions of themselves and influences how they interact with people and systems they encounter.

Educational Planning and Student Involvement

In Chapter 2, we discussed promoting self-determination in the context of the general education curriculum. Federal law and best practice in special education have always, however, emphasized the importance of an individualized education, and it is not the intent of the federal mandates for access to the general education curriculum to circumvent this. One component of receiving special education services is that a student's Individualized Education Program (IEP) is determined by an annual meeting. The IEP meeting has become a focal point for efforts to promote self-determination, and the bulk of this chapter focuses on involving students in educational planning as a means to promote self-determination. We begin, though, where the last chapter left off—providing a model for IEP teams to use to ensure that instruction to promote self-determination is determined by both the general education curriculum and a student's unique learning needs.

IEP PLANNING, ACCESS TO THE GENERAL EDUCATION CURRICULUM, AND SELF-DETERMINATION

Individualization is a hallmark of special education practices (Turnbull, Turnbull, Wehmeyer, & Park, 2003). The Individuals With Disabilities Education Act (IDEA) requires that a student's IEP be based on both the general curriculum and the student's unique learning needs. Turnbull,

Turnbull, and Wehmeyer (2006) developed an IEP team decision-making model, depicted in Figure 3.1, that assists IEP teams to achieve this. It is a given that someone on the team, and hopefully more than just one person, is familiar with the general education curriculum relevant to the student's grade level and can identify where, within the standards, self-determination

Figure 3.1   Decision-Making Model for IEP Teams

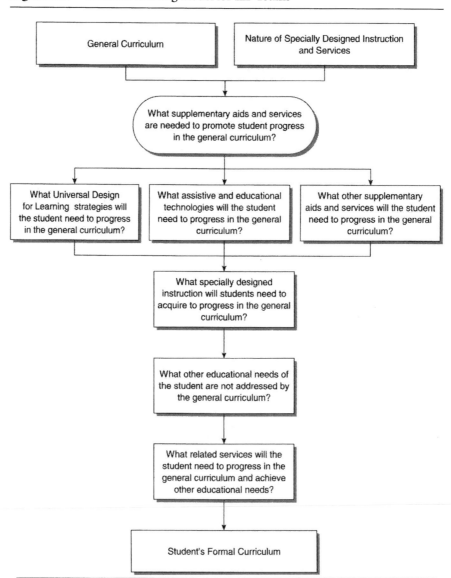

SOURCE: Wehmeyer, M. L. (2000). *Access to the general curriculum for high school students with mental retardation: Curriculum adaptation, augmentation and alteration.* Unpublished grant proposal.

topics can be addressed. It is also assumed that the IEP team has knowledge about a student's instructional needs pertaining to self-determination, a process discussed later in this chapter.

Supplementary Aids and Services

The process begins with consideration of the supplementary aids and services a student needs to promote progress in the general education curriculum, in this case, to make progress on content related to self-determination that is embedded in the general education curriculum. IDEA defines supplementary aids and services as "aids, services, and other supports that are provided in general education classes or other education related settings to enable children with disabilities to be educated with nondisabled children to the maximum extent appropriate" [20 U.S.C. 1401, SEC. 602, Page 118 Stat. 2658 (33)]. Wehmeyer (2000) identified six domains of supplementary aids and services that promote access to the general education curriculum (Table 3.1): Universal Design for Learning (UDL); access factors; classroom ecological variables; educational and assistive technology; assessment and task modifications; and teacher, paraprofessional, or peer support.

As you can see from Table 3.1, we have already discussed the first of these domains, UDL. The IEP team members should examine ways that universal design and curriculum modifications can be incorporated into the student's educational program consistent with the discussion in Chapter 2 about how UDL and curriculum modifications can promote self-determination.

The next domain, access, refers to ensuring both physical and cognitive access to the school, classroom, and other educational environments. If students cannot be part of the life of the school, they miss important opportunities to learn self-determination skills by interacting with peers and participating in school and extracurricular activities. For example, participation in student government at the high school campus may be an excellent means for students to learn skills like problem solving, decision making, or goal setting and, as such, promote self-determination. Although there are fewer situations in which the lack of physical access prohibits participation since the passage of the Americans With Disabilities Act—which requires that public buildings, including public school buildings, be fully accessible—access issues, both cognitive and physical, may still impact a student's experiences and opportunities. For example, many auditoriums in older high schools have been retrofitted to provide accessible seating, but this is often in the back of the auditorium. If student government meetings are held in such auditoria, students with physical impairments may be physically isolated, if not excluded. Teams should

Table 3.1   Supplementary Aids and Services to Ensure Access to the General Education Curriculum

Domain	Definition	Examples
Universal Design for Learning	Modifications to the way curriculum is presented or represented or to the ways in which students respond to the curriculum	Digital talking book formats, advance organizers, video or audio input/output
Access	Modifications to the community, campus, building, or classroom to ensure physical and cognitive access	Curb cuts, wide doors, clear aisles, nonprint signage
Classroom Ecology	Modifications to and arrangements of features of the classroom environment that impact learning	Seating arrangement, types of seating, acoustics, lighting
Educational and Assistive Technology	Technology that reduces the impact of a person's impairment on his or her capacity	Calculator, augmentative communication device, computer
Assessment and Task Modifications	Modifications to time or task requirements (but not content or material) to assist in participation in assessment or educational task	Extended time, scribe, notetaker, oral presentation
Teacher, Paraprofessional, or Peer Support	Support from another person to participate in instructional activities	Peer buddy, paraeducator, teacher

SOURCE: Wehmeyer, M. L. (2000). *Access to the general curriculum for high school students with mental retardation: Curriculum adaptation, augmentation and alteration.* Unpublished grant proposal.

consider what access issues are needed to ensure that students with disabilities participate fully in the life of the school. Similar issues exist with regard to classroom ecological variables, and Chapter 4 discusses these issues as they pertain to promoting self-determination in greater detail.

Next, teams need to consider how technology can promote access to the general education curriculum. For many students, access to technology, both assistive and electronic and information technologies, can play a significant role in promoting self-determination. Traditional augmentative communication devices can enable someone who has limited verbal skills to communicate their wants, needs, and preferences—an obviously important aspect of being self-determined. For students with cognitive disabilities, accessible technology can greatly diminish dependency on others. For example, one area of dependence for many students with cognitive impairments is financial planning and management. Students with mental retardation may not be able to do the math required to prepare a budget and maintain a checking account. With the advent of software programs such as Intuit's Quicken or Microsoft Money, however, the requirements for maintaining a checkbook register and budgeting change, from having to possess math skills to being able to input data and use the software. Moreover, with the capacity to download one's monthly bank statement directly from a bank Web site into Quicken or other such software, data entry becomes unnecessary.

Similarly, Ward and Meyer (1999) discussed the emergence of self-advocacy and support groups by and for people with autism largely as a function of the emergence of widely accessible e-mail and Web-based technology, where people who had difficulty communicating in other mediums were able to effectively communicate their feelings as well as learn from others with shared experiences. Such technologies hold significant promise to support some students with autism in expressing themselves, their preferences, and their choices.

Finally, with regard to supplementary aids and services, teams should consider the role of others in the student's educational setting—paraeducators, peers, and the special educator—in promoting self-determination. We discuss many of these issues in subsequent chapters that detail teacher, student, and peer-mediated instruction to promote self-determination, but it is worth making special mention here of the role of paraeducators in supporting self-determination. The role of paraeducators in the education of students with cognitive disabilities is important. Paraeducators often provide direct instruction to students, assist with group instruction situations, or work to facilitate a student's inclusion and foster the student's social network. If done well, these can enhance student self-determination. Turnbull et al. (2006) have noted, though, that in some cases, paraeducators become a source of dependency creation and instead of promoting greater independence, foster greater dependence. Turnbull and colleagues refer to this as a "Velcroed" situation, where, like Velcro, the student is never detached from the paraeducator and thus does not learn to act more autonomously. Including paraeducators as part of the IEP team and the discussion pertaining to promoting self-determination is a first step in preventing this. Additionally, as we discuss in Chapter 6, promoting student-directed learning enhances self-determination, and both paraeducators and teachers can implement and support these instructional strategies.

Specially Designed Instruction

Returning to Figure 3.1, once the IEP team has considered supplementary aids and services that promote self-determination, they need to consider the specially designed instruction necessary to promote self-determination within the context of the general education curriculum. IDEA defines special education services as "specially designed instruction," which refers to the adaptation of content, methodology, or delivery of instruction to address the unique needs of a student with a disability to ensure access to the general education curriculum. We discuss the instructional methods and strategies to promote self-determination in Chapters 5 and 6.

Other Educational Needs

As we mentioned previously, it was not the intent of the IDEA access to the general education curriculum mandates that a student's educational program be driven entirely and exclusively by the general education curriculum. Considering supplementary aids and services and specially designed instruction to promote self-determination within the context of the general education curriculum is the first step in designing an IEP that promotes self-determination. The next step is to consider what is not in the general education curriculum on which students need instruction to enhance self-determination.

One such focus will be engaging students themselves in the educational planning process, discussed next in this chapter, but it is quite likely that in most states or districts it will not be feasible to link instruction across all of the component elements listed in Table 1.1. One such area that is of particular importance is that of self-advocacy. Because self-advocacy and student involvement in educational planning are closely linked, we describe instructional efforts to promote self-advocacy in this chapter.

SELF-ADVOCACY AND STUDENT INVOLVEMENT IN EDUCATIONAL PLANNING

Promoting Self-Advocacy

Self-advocacy skills are critically important if students with disabilities are to become independent, self-determined young people and if they

Table 3.2   Instructional Areas for Self-Advocacy

Assertive Behavior

Public Speaking Skills

Leadership and Teamwork Skills

Active Listening Skills

Decision-Making Skills

Problem Resolution Skills

Legal and Citizenship Rights and Responsibilities

Transition Planning

Goal Setting and Attainment

Using Community Resources

Communication, Negotiation, and Compromise

are to participate meaningfully in their educational planning and decision-making process. Table 3.2 lists instructional areas that will enable young people to become effective self-advocates.

Assertive Behavior

Teaching students to be assertive is a logical first step in promoting self-advocacy. Assertive behavior refers to skills that enable students to express their wants, needs, and opinions honestly and openly in a way that enables them to stand up for themselves and to achieve desired goals. An instructional emphasis to promote assertive behavior incorporates a number of key elements. Teach students that assertive behavior exists on a continuum between passive behavior and aggressive behavior. Emphasize to students that "to advocate" means to speak up for, and that assertiveness and advocating go hand in hand. Specific behaviors that can be taught to students include the following:

- Make eye contact with the person who is speaking or to whom you are speaking.
- Speak with a firm, clear, and direct voice; avoid being emotional.
- Know what you are seeking and identify the right person to speak to.
- Know your rights and responsibilities.
- Be persistent.

Like many self-advocacy skill areas, the educational planning process presents an ideal circumstance in which to teach and practice assertiveness skills.

Communication Skills

Teaching effective communication skills that enable students to advocate for themselves and achieve desired outcomes goes hand in hand with teaching assertiveness skills. There are a variety of communication skills that can contribute to that outcome, including teaching students to be active listeners, to be persuasive, and to negotiate and compromise.

Listening. Students should learn that listening skills may be as important to self-advocacy as assertiveness or conversation skills. Emphasize the importance of active listening, and teach students the following:

- Look at the person who is speaking. Stress that when someone looks at a person while that person is speaking, it tells the speaker that he or she is listening to what they have to say.
- Ask questions. Emphasize that when a person is actively listening, the speaker is likely to say something that he or she can ask a question about. Questions can clarify something the speaker has said or confirm a speaker's statement. In both cases, the listener can gather more information and, at the same time, let the speaker know that he or she is listening.
- Don't interrupt. While it is a good idea to ask some questions to show that one is listening, it is a bad idea to continually interrupt the speaker. A good listener lets another person speak without interrupting unless it is really necessary. Repeated interruptions send a message to the speaker that the listener does not really want to hear what he or she has to say.
- Take notes. In some circumstances, it is appropriate to take notes. Note taking can assist the listener to remember what he or she learned in the conversation and, once more, lets the speaker know that he or she is listening. Further, if a student is having a hard time attending to the speaker, jotting down key points can help keep the student aware of the thread of the discussion.

Nonverbal Communication Skills

Nonverbal behaviors, like eye contact, facial expressions, gestures, and body language, are important components of communicative interactions, particularly communicative interactions focused on advocacy. There are a number of aspects of nonverbal communication that can be emphasized to students.

- Eye contact. Eye contact can be used to communicate a wide array of human emotions, from admiration and respect to anxiety and anger. Students can be taught to discriminate between messages sent by types of eye contact. For example, making frequent eye contact and having one's eyes open wide with raised eyebrows indicate acceptance, approval, or assertiveness. Alternatively, squinting or glaring and frequently averting eye contact can indicate disapproval, and avoiding eye contact, looking down, or staring blankly indicates indifference.
- Facial expressions. Facial expressions work in conjunction with eye contact to communicate emotions. A smile transmits feelings of approval and happiness, a frown communicates unhappiness or dissatisfaction, and anger is communicated by pursed or tightly closed lips, clenched teeth, and scowls.
- Gestures and body movements. Arm and hand motions can be used to augment verbal messages. Approval or acceptance can be expressed by head nodding, an open stance (e.g., legs uncrossed, arms at side), orienting one's body toward the other person, and other body movements or gestures. Shaking one's head from side to side, folded arms, and physical distance all express disapproval. Pointing or shaking a finger at a person, getting too close, or thrusting one's chin out can indicate aggression, and leaning away from a person, folding one's hands behind one's back, and tapping one's feet indicate indifference or boredom.

Persuasion. To persuade means to win someone over to your perspective or plan through reason and argument. In most cases, persuasion is used to convince someone that one's own plan or idea is superior to another's plan or idea to achieve a similar goal or outcome. Teaching students how to be persuasive involves teaching a series of communication strategies.

- First, acknowledge to someone that you are trying to persuade that you understand what they said or their position on a topic or issue.
- Next, explain how your plan or idea achieves the same goals as those inherent in the other person's position.
- Third, explain the additional benefits or advantages of your plan or idea.

Negotiation and compromise. A closely related set of skills involves negotiating to reach an agreed-on plan, action, or position. The goal of persuasion is to convince others that one's own plan or action is best—to have them come to your side, as it were. The goal of negotiation is not to persuade people to adopt your plan, idea, or position wholly, but instead to work out an acceptable compromise that is satisfactory to all parties.

- Teach students that to negotiate means, in essence, to work out a deal and that deals involve compromise, that is, giving up on something they want.
- Emphasize that in some cases, it is better to get some of what they want if the alternative (not compromising) means that they don't get anything of what they want.
- Teach students to identify, in advance of the negotiation, what features of their plan, idea, or proposal they would not be willing to give up.
- Tell students to begin by listening carefully to what the other person wants; then identify some aspect that they can give the other person immediately.
- Advise students to avoid becoming emotional, to keep communications positive, and to stay focused on finding areas for agreement and compromise.

Rights and Responsibilities

Because a rights expression is the core element of any assertive statement, it stands to reason that students with disabilities should learn about rights and identify the responsibilities that accompany them. Strategies to teach assertive behavior, like assertiveness training or social skills programs, focus on teaching students how to be assertive. Instruction in rights and responsibilities turns the focus toward the issue of what to advocate or assert.

Often instruction on rights focuses solely on citizenship training—for example, voting skills, understanding the Constitution, and knowledge of laws and the legislative process. This is important, certainly, and is usually embedded within the general education curriculum. More specifically, though, students with disabilities should learn about their rights as citizens with disabilities and the legal protections assured through that. This would be a good point in time to talk about issues pertaining to discrimination and equal rights protections, such as those embodied in the Americans With Disabilities Act and IDEA. Students can learn about the requirements of the IEP process, the role of various members, and the intent of the process.

Students need to further understand that rights are coupled with responsibilities and that others have rights that may, in some ways, conflict with their own rights. Students should understand that just because they have a certain right, or indeed, just because they view something as a right, does not give them a free ticket to do as they please or mean that others will recognize that right. It is for this reason that skills like negotiation and compromise, effective elaboration (acknowledging others' rights, etc.), and effective verbal and nonverbal communication are important.

Student Involvement in Educational Planning

The 1997 amendments to IDEA included language requiring that students with disabilities be invited to IEP planning meetings if transition goals are to be discussed. As a result, there has now been increased focus on engaging students in transition and education planning as a means to promote self-determination. Because the educational planning process is goal focused, involves problem solving and decision making, and provides opportunities for learning and practicing self-advocacy skills, it is a powerful and logical means to promote self-determination.

Table 3.3 shows a number of available programs designed to involve students with disabilities in their IEP meeting and planning. In 2002, the National Information Center for Children and Youth With Disabilities developed a set of materials that included a student guide to the IEP process (McGahee-Kovac, 2002) and an accompanying teacher and parent technical assistance guide (National Information Center for Children and Youth With Disabilities, 2002), both of which are available for download at http://www.nichcy.org. Although these programs differ in some ways, they address common themes and issues, discussed in this section.

We would note, though, before describing practices linked exclusively to the IEP, that some schools have adopted the practice of student-led meetings for all students, not just students with disabilities. Biannual parent-teacher conferences are a common occurrence, particularly in elementary schools, and it is quite simple and surprisingly powerful to have the child lead one of those meetings, reporting on his or her areas of achievement and areas of focus for the remainder of the school year.

IEP Process and Rights Information

Most programmatic efforts to promote student involvement begin with an overview of the IEP and the educational planning process. This often is within the broader context of explaining about transition and transition services. Students can learn what an IEP is, who is supposed to

Table 3.3   Student Involvement Programs

Program	Evaluated With	Authors	Publisher
Self-Directed IEP	Students with EBD, MR	Martin, Marshall, Maxson, & Jerman (1993)	Sopris West http://www.sopriswest.com
NEXT S.T.E.P.	Students with LD	Halpern et al. (2000)	PRO-ED, Inc. http://www.proedinc.com
Whose Future Is It Anyway?	Students with EBD, LD, OHI, MR	Wehmeyer et al. (2004)	Beach Center on Disability University of Kansas http://www.beachcenter.org
The Self-Advocacy Strategy	Students with LD	Van Reusen, Bos, Schumaker, & Deshler (2002)	Edge Enterprises P.O. Box 1304 Lawrence, KS 66044
TAKE CHARGE for the Future	Students with EBD, LD, OHI	Powers, Ellison, Matuszewski, & Turner (2004)	Portland State University Regional Research Institute for Human Services http://www.rri.pdx.edu/index.php
A Student's Guide to the IEP	No formal evaluation; designed for students across disability categories	McGahee-Kovac (2002)	National Information Center for Children and Youth With Disabilities http://www.nichcy.org

NOTE: EBD, emotional behavioral disorder; IEP, Individualized Education Program; LD, learning disability; MR, mental retardation; OHI, Other Health Impaired.

attend IEP meetings, the purpose of the IEP, and the IEP meeting process. Providing a student with a copy of his or her current IEP and going through some of the required sections (e.g., present level of performance, goals and objectives, or special education and related services) can provide learning opportunities related to self- and disability awareness, goal setting, and student interests and preferences.

If you do use this as an entry point to discuss disability issues (and this can occur because to be eligible as a member of a protected class under disability-specific laws, a person has to be a person with a disability), focus not on requiring a student to accept labels but dealing with issues pertaining to the uniqueness of every human and how a student's disability will introduce some unique learning needs. When the focus is on student learning needs, it can focus on supports and accommodations and not on labels and stigma associated with labels.

The purpose of IEP meetings. Students may have limited experiences with meetings, so focusing some instruction on types of meetings and their purposes is important. Wehmeyer et al. (2004) identified several reasons to hold meetings, particularly educational planning meetings, that can be taught to students:

1. Meetings are a good way to share information about something of interest to a lot of people. In the case of educational planning meetings, that information involves the student's educational progress, needs, and program.

2. Meetings are an effective way to build unity and establish teamwork. Educational planning meetings provide an opportunity to identify areas of mutual interest and build a team to achieve some common objectives.

3. Meetings provide an opportunity to bring people together to examine and solve a problem. No matter how effective any given person is at problem solving, it is often useful to have more than one person looking at a problem to make sure that all options are identified.

4. Meetings provide a good context in which to come to decisions that have support across stakeholders and that meet the various needs of participants.

Types of meetings. There are different kinds or types of meetings that students may encounter, both in school and as adults. These different meeting types also have differing expectations and intentions and require different skills, or more precisely, differential use of various leadership skills. Wehmeyer et al. (2004) identified these types of meetings and their purposes (see Table 3.4).

The responsibilities of participants and leaders in each type of meeting vary greatly, as do the responsibilities of meeting participants. Educational planning meetings are, essentially, decision-making meetings, in which participants have the opportunity to contribute and to share in decision-making and planning activities. Educational planning meetings provide chances for students to put into practice the leadership and teamwork skills they have acquired. A number of the programs emphasize students' running the IEP meeting.

Table 3.4   Types of Meetings

Meeting Type	Primary Purpose
Ritualistic Meeting	Usually designed to promote cohesiveness within an organization. The purpose of the meeting is to assure participants that there is adequate leadership in place and, often, to rubber-stamp decisions that have already been made.
Briefing Meeting	Designed to provide participants with information to carry out plans that are already in place.
Instructional Meeting	Designed to teach people in order to make them more proficient at their assigned tasks.
Consultative Meeting	Designed to enable a person responsible for the meeting to elicit advice and direction from meeting participants. Participants are often experts or consultants. The meeting organizer remains responsible for the decision.
Decision-Making Meeting	Designed to make decisions and formulate a course of action. Participants should be involved in problem solving, decision making, and eventually, plans to put decisions into action.

Running a meeting. The basic skills required to run an efficient decision-making meeting involve getting a meeting started, keeping participants on track, moving the meeting along, and enabling participants to reach a decision. Some specific skills that enable a student to achieve this include the following:

- Ask questions, particularly open-ended questions that cannot be answered with a simple yes or no. A student may want to start a meeting with a brief set of comments on which to base such questions.
- Set an agenda that keeps the tasks at a manageable level, and stick with the agenda and the timeline linked to that agenda.
- Summarize issues as they are discussed, identify options that arise from such discussions, and assist the group in actually making a decision.

Many students with disabilities will not be very adept at these types of skills (though some will), but that does not mean they cannot lead their IEP meeting. Martin, Marshall, Maxson, and Jerman (1993) provided an example of how a student might take a leadership role in his or her educational planning meeting. Table 3.5 identifies 11 steps in which a student could receive instruction in order to assume a leadership role in his or her planning meeting.

Table 3.5   Steps to Student Leadership of Planning Meeting

Step Number	Activity
1	Begin meeting by stating purpose.
2	Introduce everyone.
3	Review past goals and performance.
4	Ask for others' feedback.
5	State your school and transition goals.
6	Ask questions if you don't understand.
7	Deal with differences in opinion.
8	State what support you'll need.
9	Summarize your goals.
10	Close meeting by thanking everyone.
11	Work on IEP goals all year!

SOURCE: Adapted from Martin, J. E., Marshall, L., Maxson, L. L., & Jerman, P. (1993). *Self-directed IEP.* Longmont, CO: Sopris West.

Leadership and Teamwork Skills

Too often youth with disabilities are not seen as potential leaders, and the first goal of instruction is to give students a sense of what constitutes a leader. Table 3.6 provides characteristics of leaders that can be used to communicate what leaders are and do. Specific skills instruction to promote leadership will focus on individual skill components like teaching students how to set goals, resolve conflicts, be assertive, foster teamwork and participation, communicate effectively, or run a meeting, all of which we have touched on here or address in subsequent chapters. These skills can be taught using a social skills training model or employing procedures like modeling, role playing, or behavioral rehearsal.

Teamwork and participation skills. One important role of a leader is to promote teamwork and effective participation skills. Students need to

Table 3.6   Characteristics of Leaders

Leaders:

- Locate and use resources that will be of benefit to the individual or group
- Communicate effectively with the group and the public
- Help the group describe and communicate a common goal, objective, or vision
- Understand group and individual needs
- Are goal oriented, organized, and have strategic planning skills
- Set an example for others
- Teach and mentor others
- Facilitate teamwork and cooperation
- Provide feedback and evaluation
- Resolve conflicts and solve problems
- Direct group activities and equitably distribute resources and responsibilities

learn to be both effective team members and participants and, in the role of leader, to facilitate teamwork and participation. The goal of teamwork building is to get all participants working together to achieve a common objective or goal. The goal of participation skills building is to get each individual involved and contributing.

The traits of effective team members include the following:

- Have a positive attitude about the team process, trust and rely on other team members, and approach issues in a problem-solving mode.
- Follow through on what they promise.
- Make sure that they get the information they need to contribute by talking to other team members and doing their homework.

Students should learn that they can be a good team member at meetings by doing the following:

- Getting to the meeting on time
- Dressing neatly and appropriately
- Bringing any information that has been sent to them
- Working positively with other team members
- Staying throughout the meeting
- Listening without interrupting
- Talking only about the topic under discussion
- Following through on their commitments

Good participant skills and effective teamwork skills have considerable overlap. Participation skills usually focus on the team member's ability to contribute to the discussion and the decision-making/problem-solving process as a whole. Thus teaching students to be more effective decision makers or problem solvers, as we discuss in Chapter 5, will increase their participation skills. Likewise, effective communication skills, as discussed in the previous section, contribute to more effective participation skills.

Group dynamics skills. Group dynamics skills are the skills one has to use to work successfully with groups and to enable individuals within a group to work successfully together. While skills like goal setting, decision making, problem solving, and assertiveness receive the largest share of attention as leadership skills, there are a number of skills that fall under the category of group dynamics skills that may be as important. Among these are

- Active listening
- Providing reassurance and approval
- Guiding group members
- Motivating the group and modeling enthusiasm

If a group seems continually off track, confused, or if members feel that their time is being wasted, the leader needs to step in and suggest an alternative means of achieving the common objective, examine the work allocation and redistribute work if necessary, and provide a specific agenda for further action.

Conflict resolution skills. One of the more difficult challenges to teamwork that a leader must address is conflict in a group. Conflicts arise for a variety of reasons, from personality clashes to power grabs. However, one common feature of conflicts, regardless of origin, is that they are disruptive to effective teamwork and must be addressed by effective leaders. The first response to conflict on the part of the leader is to make sure that it is not a result of ineffective leadership. Leaders should examine the degree to which they have fostered good participation skills, communicated a common purpose or objective, and fostered teamwork. Given that the conflict has not been manufactured by ineffective leadership, Guerra, Moore, and Slaby (1995) provided a series of steps students could learn (in a self-directed manner) that would enable them to resolve conflicts.

- Why is there a conflict? Check facts and beliefs. Students should learn the importance of obtaining the factual information necessary to resolve the conflict and to explore their own beliefs about a situation.

- The other's perspective. Students need to learn to think about a conflict situation from the perspective of all parties in order to craft a response that will resolve the conflict to the satisfaction of everyone involved.
- Think of solutions. Based on the information gathered in the first two steps, students need to learn to generate possible solutions to the problem.
- Decide on a solution. Students should apply decision-making skills to identify the most satisfactory solution to the conflict. At this point in the process, students will need to employ effective negotiation, compromise, and persuasion skills as well.
- Evaluate results. Once a conflict has been resolved, students need to learn to monitor ongoing interactions and keep a similar situation from boiling up again.

Goal-Setting, Problem-Solving, and Decision-Making Skills

If the steps in the conflict resolution process just described seem eerily familiar, it is because it is essentially just a problem-solving process. Solving problems, making decisions, and setting goals form the core of instructional efforts to promote student involvement in educational planning and decision making. Because we discuss instructional strategies pertaining to each of these content areas in Chapters 5 and 6, we will not go into any depth with regard to these in this chapter, other than to note how these have been dealt with specifically in the IEP planning context.

Several programs have created mnemonics to assist students to implement these critical skills in the IEP context. For example, Van Reusen, Bos, Schumaker, and Deshler (2002) developed the I PLAN mnemonic, depicted in Table 3.7, to help students organize the goal-setting process linked to

Table 3.7   I PLAN Steps for a Successful Transition Meeting

Initial	Activity
I	Inventory your strengths, areas to improve or learn, and goals and choices for learning or accommodations.
P	Provide your inventory information.
L	Listen and respond.
A	Ask questions.
N	Name your goals.

Table 3.8   DO IT! Process for Problem Solving

Initial	Activity
D	**D**efine the problem.
O	**O**utline your options.
I	**I**dentify the outcome of each option.
T	**T**ake action.
!	Get excited!

SOURCE: Wehmeyer, M., Lawrence, M., Kelchner, K., Palmer, S., Garner, N., & Soukup, J. (2004). *Whose future is it anyway? A student-directed transition planning process* (2nd ed.). Lawrence, KS: Beach Center on Disability.

the IEP. Similarly, Wehmeyer et al. (2004) used the DO IT! mnemonic, depicted in Table 3.8, to help students remember a simple problem-solving strategy to apply to transition planning.

The technical assistance guide published by the National Information Center for Children and Youth With Disabilities (2002) provides some additional recommendations:

- Start working with students in the beginning of the year.
- Tailor working with the IEP to the needs and abilities of each student. Not every student will be able to write his or her own entire IEP, but all should—and can—participate in some fashion. With some students, you may want to concentrate on only some of the IEP sections or on inviting and facilitating their participation in the process (e.g., describing strengths and interests, describing the disability, listing the accommodations that are needed, talking about future plans).
- Realize that this undertaking requires a commitment of time. Your students will certainly benefit, and they are sure to surprise their teachers, parents, and even themselves. However, be aware that talking to students about IEPs and helping them prepare for the IEP meeting will take time.
- Start slowly, devoting time each week to talking with students about themselves and their IEPs. Talk weekly with students about their strengths, needs, learning differences, academic goals, and plans for the future. Work with them via worksheets, class discussion, individualized work, and role playing. By slowly building a foundation and progressively building on it, this work will not seem too overwhelming or in-depth for students.

- Always tailor discussions and work to the needs and capabilities of your students, but don't underestimate them. As you well know, they can surprise you with their ideas, their understanding, and their desire and ability to participate and speak up for themselves.
- Celebrate each student's strengths and growth! (pp. 14–15)

The IEP planning process provides a unique and powerful context within which to teach and practice self-determination skills, and at some level or another, every student can and should be involved in his or her educational planning.

Schoolwide and Classroom Ecological Interventions

I f students are to become more self-determined, it is important that they receive explicit instruction in the knowledge, skills, and beliefs associated with self-determination. The degree to which students are able to acquire and practice knowledge, skills, and beliefs leading to enhanced self-determination will be affected by the support and opportunities provided to promote self-determination throughout the school and within the classroom as well as by the direct instruction students receive. Too frequently, students with disabilities (and students without disabilities) do not have adequate opportunities to learn and practice how to be self-determined, and they find themselves in settings that are unresponsive to their efforts to be self-determined (Wall & Dattilo, 1995). In this chapter, we discuss the schoolwide and classroom-based factors that affect opportunities to learn and express self-determination, such as school culture and climate and classroom management issues.

As we discussed in Chapter 1, a self-determination emphasis within the education of students with disabilities will be most successful if it is implemented within the context of the general education curriculum and classroom. This does not mean that some competencies promoting self-determination cannot be taught within specialized settings. Instruction to promote the knowledge, skills, and beliefs leading to enhanced self-determination should be taught to students independent of the setting in which they receive their educational program. As we indicated earlier, though, there are a number of reasons that efforts to promote student self-determination will be most successful if they occur within the context of the general education classroom with an awareness of the importance of schoolwide issues that are important to self-determination.

Many schoolwide and classroom factors affect the ability of students to develop and express self-determination (Field & Hoffman, 2002a). To frame your consideration of these issues, we have identified a number of quality indicators that can be used as a self-assessment of your school and classroom efforts to promote self-determination. These are listed in Table 4.1.

Table 4.1 Quality Indicators of Schoolwide and Classroom Factors That Support the Development of Self-Determination

---

Quality Indicator #1: Knowledge, skills, and attitudes for self-determination are addressed in the curriculum, in family support programs, and in staff development.

Quality Indicator #2: Students, parents, and staff are involved participants in individualized educational decision making and planning.

Quality Indicator #3: Students, families, faculty, and staff are provided with opportunities for choice.

Quality Indicator #4: Students, families, faculty, and staff are encouraged to take appropriate risks.

Quality Indicator #5: Supportive relationships are encouraged.

Quality Indicator #6: Accommodations and supports for individual needs are provided.

Quality Indicator #7: Students, families, and staff have the opportunity to express themselves and be understood.

Quality Indicator #8: Consequences for actions are predictable.

Quality Indicator #9: Self-determination is modeled through the school environment.

In Resource A, we have provided a copy of the Self-Determination Quality Indicators Assessment Tool. This tool is intended to assist you in your assessment of the presence of these quality indicators in your school and classroom. To inventory the present level of a school's or program's performance relative to the self-determination quality indicators, team members should identify ways they are and are not meeting the standard for each indicator. It may also be helpful for teams to rate the degree to which they think an indicator is being implemented in their setting on a scale of 1 to 4. If a numerical rating is used, it is a good idea for team members to assign ratings to each indicator individually first and then come together as a team to discuss their ratings and arrive at a team consensus rating. Alternatively, teams may choose to rate each item through group discussion.

Before discussing these specifically, we would note a few issues that are overarching. First, an emphasis on promoting the self-determination of all members of the school community (students, parents, faculty, administrators, and staff) is evident throughout the list of indicators. This emphasis on self-determination for all members of the school community promotes students' learning about self-determination through role modeling provided by others within the environment and by creating a collegial community for learning. The models provided within students' environments, positive or negative, greatly affect students' development of skills promoting self-determination. Therefore, it is important to promote self-determination for all members of the school community to ensure that students' role models demonstrate positive learning experiences about self-determination.

This commitment to self-determination for all often begins with the establishment of a schoolwide or campus-level mission or vision that emphasizes that all children are part of the school community and that desired outcomes, such as student success, citizenship, and creating lifelong learners, apply to all students, including students with disabilities.

In a study of schools that were actively working to promote self-determination, Eisenman and Chamberlin (2001) found that participating teachers and administrators emphasized the importance of special and general educators working together to promote self-determination throughout the school. Eisenman and Chamberlin elaborated on this concept with the following statement:

> Participants believed that approaching self-determination as something to be done by special educators for special education students would encourage fragmented and isolated efforts within schools and ultimately undermine broad support for their work, which is a common result of many educational innovations (Fullan & Miles, 1992). They believed that their colleagues would agree with the importance of encouraging self-determination for all students, given the opportunity to discuss its constituent elements and identify the elements already embedded or most relevant to their own curricular areas and instructional approaches. They realized that change in this direction would be most likely to occur if they developed shared understandings and goals with their colleagues. (p. 143)

Eisenman and Chamberlin (2001) also observed that school staff members, including administrators and general, vocational, and special education teachers, needed time to discuss the concept of self-determination and how it relates to what they do in their school and classrooms. You may need to be a catalyst for this type of conversation. Perhaps the conduct of the curriculum mapping process discussed in Chapter 2 would be an appropriate time in which to bring up these issues.

The steps in the model of self-determination proposed by Field and Hoffman (1994), described in Chapter 1, can also guide teachers and planning teams to examine the school and classroom factors that promote self-determination. These steps can also contribute to the empowerment evaluation process discussed in Chapter 7.

Know yourself and the environment and value yourself. In the context of the educational program development process, knowing yourself involves assessing the current strengths and weaknesses of your programmatic efforts related to promoting self-determination. The Self-Determination Quality Indicators Assessment Tool can provide a means to do this, and we discuss specific issues pertaining to each quality indicator subsequently. Valuing yourself focuses on believing in the importance of the school community members, the program, and the concept of self-determination enough to initiate and sustain the development of an emphasis on self-determination.

Plan. After teams have developed greater self-awareness of the strengths and limitations of their programmatic efforts and have established a belief in the importance of their role in supporting student self-determination, they need to set goals and plan actions to meet those goals. Again, the Self-Determination Quality Indicators Assessment Tool can be used to identify areas in which programmatic goals are most important. Such goals should focus on ensuring high-quality instruction on knowledge and skills pertaining to self-determination, preferably within the context of the general education curriculum, as well as creating opportunities for students to practice and hone these skills and to develop the attitudes that will support them to become more self-determined. These goals may be at the classroom, school, or district level.

Act. The next step in the Field and Hoffman (1994) self-determination model is to take action. Considering the many conflicting demands that are a reality in schools today, there is a tendency for educators to become reactive rather than proactive. It is essential to develop a proactive stance and take action on the goals that are set if infusing instructional and programmatic efforts to promote self-determination is to become a reality. Getting together regularly as a team can help ensure that goals and plans are turned into action. The team can provide both support and accountability for meeting the goals.

Experience outcomes and learn. Teams need to assess their progress toward their programmatic goals on an ongoing basis and celebrate their accomplishments. They also need to set new goals based on their experiences and new knowledge they have developed. This can be accomplished within the context of the empowerment evaluation process, discussed in Chapter 7. Self-assessment of programmatic efforts to promote self-determination should be conducted on at least an annual basis after the initial inventory to provide the opportunity for ongoing and continuous self-improvement. As a program grows and changes and staff changes occur, it is important to take new readings of current progress to ensure continuous program maintenance and growth.

QUALITY INDICATORS OF PROGRAMMATIC EFFORTS

Each of the quality indicators for self-determination listed in Table 4.1 is discussed in this section, and some sample strategies for each of these indicators are provided. It is important to remember that these strategies are just examples. They are intended to provide you with some ideas and a starting point. Your efforts to promote self-determination will be most successful if you and your team use your creativity (and your self-determination!) to develop strategies that are most appropriate in your setting.

Quality Indicator #1: Knowledge, Skills, and Attitudes for Self-Determination Are Addressed in the Curriculum, in Family Support Programs, and in Staff Development

As we discuss throughout this book, any effort to promote self-determination needs to provide students, parents, and teachers throughout the school community with opportunities to learn knowledge, skills, and beliefs that will help them increase their self-determination. We cannot expect that these skills will be learned without direct instruction and support; they need to be explicitly taught. To some degree, the intent of this book is to enable you to reach this first quality indicator. As such, strategies to directly teach knowledge, skills, and beliefs leading to enhanced self-determination are the predominant focus in this book. In Chapters 5 and 6, we provide detailed information on how to help students acquire competencies that will lead to greater self-determination, and in Chapter 2, we provided suggestions pertaining to infusing instruction to promote self-determination into the general education curriculum. In Chapter 8, we address strategies to support families in applying self-determination concepts and skills to their parenting. In Chapter 9, we provide suggestions to support further development and expression of self-determination in teachers and administrators.

Some examples of schoolwide and classroom strategies that support providing direct instruction in component elements of self-determined behavior include the following:

- A framework is used to guide systematic infusion of knowledge, skills, and beliefs for self-determination in the curriculum (e.g., Field & Hoffman, 1994; Kohler & Ward, 2001; Wehmeyer, 2001).
- Faculty and staff are provided with inservice opportunities to develop skills related to self-determination, such as self-assessment of professional strengths and weaknesses, goal setting, and time management.
- Parent-to-parent support groups focused on parent advocacy are available for families.

Quality Indicator #2: Students, Parents, and Staff Are Involved Participants in Individualized Educational Decision Making and Planning

In Chapter 3, we detailed a step-by-step process by which Individualized Education Program (IEP) teams can ensure a focus on promoting self-determination within the context of the general education curriculum and addressing unique student learning needs. That process presumes that the team works actively to involve stakeholders. The IEP process provides an excellent vehicle to help students learn and practice skills leading to enhanced self-determination, as discussed in the previous chapter. It also provides an opportunity for other members of students' teams to develop a greater understanding of the role self-determination plays in those students' lives. Specific strategies for helping students further develop and express their self-determination through the IEP process were provided in Chapter 3. Ways in which parents can support their sons and daughters to be self-determined in their IEPs are provided in Chapter 8, and modeling strategies for teachers are presented in Chapter 9.

Some examples of schoolwide strategies that would positively affect opportunities for students and parents to participate in educational planning meetings include the following:

- Inviting students and parents to attend IEP meetings at times that are convenient for them and encouraging them to actively participate in those meetings (e.g., asking questions, being receptive to responses)
- Providing students with instruction to help them prepare for active participation in the IEP process
- Sending materials home to parents to increase their awareness and prepare them to discuss some of the items that will be addressed at the meeting

Quality Indicator #3: Students, Families, Faculty, and Staff Are Provided With Opportunities for Choice

Students, parents, and educators all need opportunities to practice their knowledge, skills, and beliefs pertaining to self-determination in real situations if they are to develop fluency in their ability to act in a self-determined manner. Learning by experience in real settings is highly important to effective learning (Bandura, 1986). Therefore, it is important that the opportunity for all school community members to model and practice self-determination skills be available in order to enhance development of students' knowledge, beliefs, and skills related to self-determination. This can be done only if opportunities for choice are available. Examples of ways in which school community members can be provided opportunities to make choices include the following:

- Encouraging students to participate in course selection
- Providing opportunities for students to choose from several options as to how they will complete class assignments
- Providing families with options from which they can choose for conference times
- Supporting families to make choices and have meaningful input in the educational decision-making process
- Encouraging faculty and staff to express preferences, choose from multiple options, and negotiate regarding teaching assignments and other duties
- Providing opportunities for faculty to select curriculum materials from a wide variety of options

Quality Indicator #4: Students, Families, Faculty, and Staff Are Encouraged to Take Appropriate Risks

Acting in a self-determined manner involves taking risks. Being self-determined is not only about thinking about what you want to do. It involves taking action. Whenever we take action, there is some element of risk involved. An environment that embraces a focus on promoting self-determination will encourage appropriate risk taking. Trying out new actions and learning from the results of those actions is part of what learning and self-determination are all about. A community that supports self-determination will encourage its participants to try new things and learn from their experiences.

Individuals within the school community need to be encouraged to take calculated risks. By calculated risks, we mean those for which the individual has adequately prepared. Instruction should be provided on how potential negative consequences of intended actions can be minimized by preparatory strategies such as considering potential consequences to actions before acting and breaking large goals into small, double steps with minimal risk (e.g., baby steps). Furthermore, safety nets need to be established so that individuals have the opportunity to recover from actions that did not result in the outcomes they were hoping for.

Some examples of ways that appropriate risk taking can be encouraged throughout the school include the following:

- Providing students with an opportunity to explore coursework and career opportunities that are new to them
- Encouraging families to suggest and experiment with new strategies at home to support the accomplishment of educational objectives
- Using the staff development and the supervision and evaluation process to encourage teachers to try out new teaching strategies

Quality Indicator #5: Supportive Relationships Are Encouraged

Several studies conducted with adults with and without disabilities in a wide variety of occupations and with students, both with and without disabilities, have found that developing supportive relationships with others is central to developing a greater sense of self-determination (Eisenman & Chamberlin, 2001; Field, Hoffman, & Fullerton, 2002; Field, Hoffman, Sawilowsky, & St. Peter, 1996a, 1996b; Ryan & Deci, 2000). For example, Field et al. (1996a) asked adults who were employed and working in the community, "What is the greatest support to self-determination?" The most frequent response was "other people," and often the other person mentioned was a family member. Conversely, when the same individuals were asked about their greatest barrier to self-determination, again the most frequent response was "other people," and often specific family members were identified. Interviews conducted by Sarver (2000) found that adults with learning disabilities in postsecondary education settings also placed a high value on the importance of relationships to supporting their self-determination. The importance of relationships to self-determination, both for providing solid emotional grounding and to help access additional resources, was affirmed in a study of self-determination of educators (Field et al., 2002). Ryan and Deci (2000) asserted that a sense of relatedness provides a secure foundation from which to become self-determined.

This emphasis on relationships is one reason we assert that efforts to promote self-determination are best pursued in the context of the general education classroom, where students with disabilities can form relationships with nondisabled peers. The type of climate that exists in a school strongly affects the types of relationships developed within that setting. Schools that develop a culture where positive relationships and communication patterns are valued are taking an important step toward fostering self-determination.

Some examples of ways that schools can promote positive relationships include the following:

- Offering peer support programs, such as peer tutoring, peer mentoring, and peer counseling, as discussed in Chapter 6
- Providing students with an opportunity to participate in cooperative learning activities; inviting family members to participate in fun, informal school activities (e.g., family fun night, receptions following school concerts)
- Using team-based teaching methods
- Implementing mentoring programs for new teachers
- Offering opportunities for parents to engage with each other socially (e.g., grade-level coffees for parents, dads' clubs, etc.)

Quality Indicator #6: Accommodations and Supports for Individual Needs Are Provided

If an environment is not accessible to individuals who are endeavoring to learn and express a sense of self-determination, they will be inhibited in their efforts to reach their goals. For example, if a student using a wheelchair chooses to take a course that is located on the second floor of a building and there is no elevator in the building, that student's ability to achieve his or her goal is obviously going to be hampered. Less obvious, but just as limiting, are barriers that may be found in academic or instructional areas. For example, if parents have difficulty with written material and all of the communication that comes from the school is in written format, those parents are likely to have additional barriers to overcome to achieve what they want in relation to providing parental support for their children at school.

When we think about accommodations, we typically think of those things we do to accommodate for a person's disability, such as ramps, elevators, interpreters, extra time on tests, and so forth. However, if we take the concept of accommodation a step further and look at it as ways we arrange the environment to maximize the levels at which persons in that environment can participate in activities, we can use the concept to support all school community members to maximize their self-determination. If we have fewer barriers that we have to overcome to reach our goals, we will have more energy and resources available to us as we work toward our goals. For example, if teachers are provided with appropriate workspace, it will be easier for them to accomplish their planning and instructional goals. If a variety of times are offered for parent conferences, family members will have more energy to juggle work, family, and school schedules and have more resources left to pursue their goals.

Some examples of individual supports that promote self-determination are provided below:

- Providing accommodations necessary for students, family members, and staff members with disabilities (e.g., interpreters, modified texts, architectural features)
- Using universal design principles in instructional and architectural design
- Consulting with a parent advisory council when planning family activities and asking for input on the types of accommodations that need to be made so that families can easily participate
- Encouraging teachers to work in teams and divide work in a manner that capitalizes on each teacher's strengths

Quality Indicator #7: Students, Families, and Staff Have the Opportunity to Express Themselves and Be Understood

This is closely linked to support for positive relationships (Quality Indicator #5) and encouragement to take appropriate risks (Quality Indicator #4). A primary way we learn about ourselves (e.g., what we like and don't like, what we value, what our strengths are) is through our conversations with others. The power of being listened to and understood is the basis for many therapies, as well as the value we find in many of our friendships. Often it is through the experience of expressing our thoughts out loud, hearing others' reactions to them, and feeling understood that we are able to clarify our thinking.

Opportunities for students, staff, and families to engage in thoughtful discussions that encourage individual reflection can be infused throughout the school day. Placing an emphasis on listening can create a learning environment in which all school community members feel stronger, more respected, and more valued. These are important building blocks for increasing self-determination. It can also help students and other school community members develop valuable communication skills as they learn to listen to others.

Some examples of ways in which these opportunities can occur are provided below:

- Encouraging all students to participate in student government activities.
- Providing opportunities for dialogue among students and staff as part of class assignments. For example, when you are discussing the meaning of a passage within a novel in a language arts class, pose a question that frames the issue in terms of an issue that adolescents face today. Encourage the expression of differing points of view and support students to think about the issue from differing perspectives.
- Encouraging the expression of divergent opinions by students, families, and staff in faculty meetings, parent groups, and school improvement teams.

Quality Indicator #8: Consequences for Actions Are Predictable

A common misconception is that an emphasis on self-determination will lead to chaos in the classroom. This is based on the inaccurate notion that within a self-determination-focused educational setting, students will be encouraged to do whatever they choose to do and will not experience any negative reactions from those consequences. To the contrary, good classroom management practices that allow students to predict the likely consequences for their actions increase the degree of control students experience in the class as well as the opportunity for self-determination. In an orderly classroom, students can make informed choices about their actions and engage in actions they predict will bring about the consequences they desire. This can be used to help them build skills to predict potential consequences of their actions in other community environments as well.

In settings that promote self-determination, expectations and boundaries are explicitly stated and agreed on. There will be a stronger consensus around expectations and boundaries if all those who are expected to work within the framework of the expectations have role-appropriate input when the expectations are delineated. For example, when talking about behavioral expectations, a teacher may say that within her classroom, she expects student behavior will be such that (a) all students have the opportunity to learn, and (b) all students will be treated with respect. She might then ask the class to generate a list of behaviors or rules that would meet those two standards. In this instance, both the teacher and the students are participating in establishing the classroom expectations in a manner that is appropriate to their roles.

Some examples of strategies that support predictability in educational settings include the following:

- Having clearly delineated behavioral expectations for each classroom
- Providing a schoolwide code of conduct for students where expectations are explicitly stated
- Involving students in setting rules in classrooms
- Using students to resolve conflicts in the class or school
- Having a managerial and decision-making structure for the school that is clearly understood by students, families, faculty, and staff
- Providing a system for students to set individual goals where the students clearly understand where (e.g., which class or content) they can set their own goals, what parameters those goals must fit within (e.g., they must fit within a certain academic content, they must not violate school rules or governmental laws), and what types of support might be available to them in the pursuit of their goals

Quality Indicator #9: Self-Determination Is Modeled Throughout the School Environment

The effectiveness of modeling as a teaching strategy is emphasized throughout this book. It is important that those responsible for leadership within the school consider the implications of school and district policies and activities in terms of how they will support or interfere with providing opportunities for expressing and, as a result, modeling self-determination in the school setting by all members of the school community, students, parents, and staff.

Some examples of ways in which students and other community members might observe modeling of self-determination throughout the school include the following:

- Establishing peer mentoring and cooperative learning programs where students have the opportunity to observe the self-determined behavior of other students. These programs may include cross-age programs (e.g., high school students mentor middle school students) where some of the opportunities to observe self-determined behavior in mentors may be most obvious.
- Encouraging principals to visibly assume leadership responsibility within the school, by forthrightly addressing problems, celebrating successes, and supporting active participation by students, parents, and staff.
- Supporting teachers to assume leadership responsibility for conditions in their classrooms. Leadership responsibility could include such areas as having clearly stated expectations, addressing any problems as they arise, and actively encouraging a classroom climate where learning is valued and all students are treated with respect.
- Actively encouraging all school community members (e.g., students, parents, faculty, and staff) to be involved in the school improvement process.

Infusing instruction on component elements of self-determined behavior into the instructional program is a core component of creating a school that values and encourages self-determination. It is essential that we address school and classroom environmental issues in addition to providing direct instruction in self-determination competencies if we are to help students learn to apply those skills. Informal learning that occurs through the modeling process is highly important. If we communicate to students that self-determination is important through the instructional program, but they don't observe self-determined role models in the school, they will be receiving mixed messages at best. At worst, they will learn that what they are learning in the classroom isn't meaningful in real settings. In order for teachers and parents to model self-determination, the school culture and climate must encourage them to practice and express their own self-determination. In addition to observing role models of self-determination within the school, it is essential that students have an opportunity to apply and practice self-determination in a variety of school settings. This will provide them opportunities to generalize skills learned in the classroom and learn from real experiences. It will also provide them with an opportunity to practice their skills in a safe setting.

Teacher-Directed Instructional Strategies

If students are going to acquire the knowledge, skills, and beliefs that lead to enhanced self-determination, it is essential that they receive high-quality instruction targeted to that end. Just as we don't expect students to learn to read without instruction in reading, we can't expect students to learn the knowledge and skills they need to become more self-determined without explicit instruction in the component elements that contribute to self-determination. As discussed in Chapter 2, instruction to promote self-determination infused into the general education curriculum and classroom is the most desirable approach to promoting the self-determination of all children and youth, including children and youth with disabilities. By infusing an instructional focus on self-determination into existing courses and content areas, we are more likely to present self-determination concepts in a manner where students can easily see their application to real situations. Furthermore, teachers are not burdened with trying to fit one more thing into their already busy schedules. Finally, by integrating instruction to promote self-determination into existing academic content areas, students with and without disabilities can learn these important skills together in the general education classroom.

Instruction to promote self-determination is necessary and appropriate throughout a student's educational career, from early childhood to postsecondary education. Although most instructional interventions to promote self-determination were developed for high school students, essentially because the self-determination emphasis in special education came about through the transition from school to community movement, there are several examples of self-instruction to promote determination at the middle school level. In addition, at least three models of self-determination instruction developed specifically for elementary-age students are available. There are also curricular materials and instructional strategies available to teach self-determination skills in preschool (e.g., Serna, Nielsen, & Forness, in press) and postsecondary (e.g., Byron & Parker, 2002) settings.

In Chapter 2, we provided guidelines specific to infusing an instructional focus on promoting self-determination into four levels of instructional planning: course and unit planning, and weekly and daily planning. We also provided suggestions for designing instruction that is appropriate to meet individual needs of diverse learners within a classroom by using Universal Design for Learning (UDL) and cognitive taxonomies. In Chapters 3 and 4, we provided suggestions for promoting student involvement in educational planning and addressing classroom and school factors that affect self-determination. In this chapter, we provide specific strategies and materials for teaching competencies related to self-determination through teacher-directed instruction.

Any effort to incorporate instruction to promote self-determination into the existing curriculum should begin by assessing where self-determination content is already being delivered. The curriculum mapping process discussed in Chapter 2 illustrates one way to achieve this. Most schools find that they are already addressing many self-determination competencies, in part because of the fact that teaching component elements like goal setting, problem solving, and decision making is good for all students. However, they also typically find there are important self-determination competencies that are not being addressed in their curricula and that students do not learn how to combine the component skills so that they lead to greater self-determination. To determine your program's strengths and needs related to self-determination, you can use one of the self-determination models provided in Chapter 1 to provide the basis for a program inventory, noting which of the skills identified in the model are taught in the curriculum and which are not. In addition, you can examine your state's standards and benchmarks, as suggested in Chapter 2, to determine where self-determination instruction may already be occurring within the academic core curriculum. Remember also to examine your curriculum for elective classes and support services as well as core academic classes. For example, many counseling programs include a focus on instruction in self-determination competencies in their offerings. Some schools have found that collaborative instructional efforts by teachers and school counselors are excellent ways to provide instruction in knowledge, skills, and beliefs related to self-determination.

In a study of six programs that were identifed as placing a major emphasis on promoting self-determination for students with disabilities,

Karvonen, Test, Wood, Browder, and Algozzine (2004) found that all six of these exemplary programs used a combination of teacher-made and published curricula to teach skills leading to enhanced self-determination among their students. The approach used to promote self-determination in these exemplary programs typically followed a sequence of teachers providing information, then using modeling and role playing, and finally generalizing the taught self-determination skills to new situations. The strategies used in these programs are consistent with the cornerstones for providing self-determination instruction delineated by Field and Hoffman (1996), which placed an emphasis on the use of modeling and experiential learning to teach knowledge, skills, and beliefs for self-determination. Students learn to be self-determined by using and practicing the skills of self-determination. Therefore, it is essential that self-determination instructional efforts include experiential practice.

LEARNING PROCESS STRATEGIES

Several instructional strategies are particularly well suited to teaching knowledge, skills, and beliefs for self-determination. Some of these strategies are discussed below.

Modeling and Mentors

Modeling is one instructional strategy that has been emphasized throughout several of the self-determination model programs. The use of successful adult role models, in particular, has been strongly emphasized. Research has demonstrated that modeling is a particularly powerful instructional strategy (Bandura, 1986). Modeling can be used as a direct instructional strategy (e.g., using role models to demonstrate a specific self-determination skill) or an indirect strategy (e.g., encouraging students to learn vicariously by observing teachers and other adults in the school who consistently model behaviors associated with self-determination). Several self-determination model projects have established mentorship programs to help students further develop self-determination skills by observing adult role models. For example, in the TAKE CHARGE for the Future curriculum (Powers et al., 2004; also see Table 3.3), students are paired with mentors who have similar challenges and interests.

Cooperative Learning Groups

Forming cooperative groups where students can learn from each other also has been used in self-determination instructional efforts. Cooperative learning (a) increases the availability of peer role modeling experiences and (b) helps students learn collaboration skills. The effectiveness of cooperative learning has been well established in the literature in several classic studies (Johnson & Johnson, 1986; Johnson, Johnson, Holubec, & Roy, 1984; Johnson, Johnson, & Maruyama, 1983). One benefit of cooperative learning is that it provides an opportunity for students to learn from models provided by their peers. An additional advantage is that it helps students strengthen their communication and relationship skills, both of which have been found to be highly important competencies for enhanced self-determination.

Coaching

According to Byron and Parker (2002), coaching is a new service delivery model that has recently attracted much attention in postsecondary services for students with attention deficit hyperactivity disorders (ADHD) and learning disabilities. Coaching emerged as a model in the 1990s within corporate training settings to provide support and mentoring to help individuals achieve their goals. Organizations such as the Attention Deficit Disorder Association and the American Coaching Association adapted the corporate model to a more structured and private practice version for use with adults with ADHD. Subsequently, several higher education institutions sought training in coaching techniques and began to offer coaching to students with ADHD and learning disabilities to help them succeed in postsecondary education settings (Parker & Byron, 1998). In addition, many teachers in K–12 schools have had great interest in the model of coaching services provided in postsecondary settings and have begun to implement similar practices.

Many definitions of coaching have been provided in the literature. One of these definitions describes coaching as an intervention model that can promote self-determination:

> In a co-active coaching relationship the agenda comes from the client, not the coach. . . . The relationship is entirely focused on getting the results clients want. They set the agenda. The coach's job is to make sure the agenda doesn't get lost. . . . This is different from consulting, for example, where the consultant brings specialized expertise and very often sets the agenda for the relationships. Co-active coaching is not about the coach's content, or the coach's expertise, or giving solutions. (Whitworth, Kimsey-House, & Sandahl, 1998, as cited in Byron & Parker, 2002, pp. 336–337)

According to Byron and Parker (2002), a number of beliefs are implicit throughout the array of coaching definitions and frameworks. These include (a) using questioning as a primary communication tool, (b) working from a belief base that clients or students usually possess the capacity to develop their own solutions, (c) explicitly deciding on communication and logistical components of the coaching relationship that are mutually agreed on by the coach and the client, and (d) emphasizing the importance of breaking goals into small steps and working to achieve those goals one step at a time.

Coaching is a new model that is emerging within services for students with ADHD and learning disabilities. Few data are available about the effects of coaching, including the effects of coaching on students' self-determination. However, the concept of coaching is consistent with the basic tenets of promoting self-determination and should be considered.

Behavioral Strategies

The behavioral strategies teachers use can have a significant impact on students' acquisition and utilization of skills related to self-determination. In Chapter 6, we discuss a number of student-directed learning strategies that are derived from operant psychology and applied behavioral analysis. Reinforcement techniques that foster motivation, self-esteem, and creativity and that encourage an internal, rather than external, locus of control are recommended to promote self-determination (Field & Hoffman, 2002a). For example, positive reinforcement should be used to encourage positive behaviors, rather than using punishment to extinguish negative behaviors. A focus on self-determination also has implications for how behavioral targets are established. Principles of self-determination suggest that students be included as participants in defining desired positive behaviors. Although naturally occurring reinforcers and consequences should be maintained, behavioral strategies should also include reinforcement of behaviors that help students reach goals they identify as important to them.

Reinforcement techniques should also encourage appropriate student experimentation and risk taking. Therefore, it may be appropriate to reinforce approximations of desired behaviors, depending on the starting level for each student.

When discussing reinforcement strategies, it is important to recognize that some research suggests that an overreliance on teacher-controlled behavioral techniques tends to decrease motivation. For example, Koestner, Ryan, Bernieri, and Holt (1984), in their examination of the role of teacher versus student control on motivation and engagement in activities, set up three conditions or reinforcement. In the first condition, children were offered a reinforcer for painting pictures (contingent reinforcement). In the second condition, children were not told before they painted pictures that they would be reinforced, but they received reinforcement for painting the pictures on completion of the activity. In the third condition, no external reinforcement for painting pictures was provided. When students were given the opportunity to paint pictures at a later time, the group that had earlier been given contingent reinforcement drew significantly fewer pictures than either of the other two groups. Although the use of reinforcement can be useful in helping students acquire and maintain new behaviors, it is important to consider the potentially negative consequences of contingent reinforcement on internal motivation and thus on self-determination.

TEACHING COMPONENT ELEMENTS OF SELF-DETERMINED BEHAVIOR

As we have indicated, there are several available curricular programs or packages designed to promote self-determination. We've identified a few of these in Table 5.1, and you can learn about more at the Self-Determination Synthesis Project (SDSP) Web site (www.uncc.edu/sdsp). These curricular materials often include instructional methods and materials that address the component elements of self-determined behavior (see Table 1.1) addressed in this section. Our effort here, though, is to provide some general instructional strategies that can be used to provide instruction in these important component elements that are not linked to specific curriculum or instructional materials. If you would like specific lesson plans, we suggest that you examine some of the curriculum materials provided in Table 5.1 or on the SDSP Web site.

Teaching Goal Setting and Attainment

Research has suggested some general strategies to follow to make goals both meaningful and attainable for students. First, goals should be challenging for the student, though not be so challenging that the student cannot attain them, as this will lead to frustration and withdrawal from participation. However, they must provide enough motivation for the student to work to attain them. If goals are too easy, there is no motivation to engage in the work necessary to attain them, and there is no feeling of accomplishment after achieving them. While it is preferable for students

Table 5.1   Self-Determination Instructional Materials

Program	Description	Authors	Publisher
ChoiceMaker Curriculum	Consists of three sections: (1) Choosing Goals, (2) Expressing Goals, and (3) Taking Action. Each section contains two to four teaching goals and numerous teaching objectives addressing six transition areas. Included are (a) an assessment tool, (b) *Choosing Goals* lessons, (c) the *Self-Directed IEP* (Individualized Education Program), and (d) *Taking Action* lessons. The program includes a criterion-referenced self-determination transition assessment tool that matches the curricular sections. The *Choosing Goals* lessons enable students to learn the necessary skills and personal information needed to articulate their interests, skills, limits, and goals across one or more self-selected transition areas. The *Self-Directed IEP* lessons enable students to learn the leadership skills necessary to manage their IEP meeting and publicly disclose their interests, skills, limits, and goals identified through the *Choosing Goals* lessons.	Martin & Marshall (1995)	Sopris West Longmont, CO http://www.sopris west.com
Steps to Self-Determination (2nd ed.)	Based on a self-determination model that has five components: Know Yourself and Your Environment, Value Yourself, Plan, Act, and Experience Outcomes and Learn. It is geared toward middle and high school–age students. (An elementary version of the curriculum and a guide for *Self-Determined*	Hoffman & Field (2006)	PRO-ED, Inc. Austin, TX http://www .proedinc.com

(Continued)

Table 5.1 (Continued)

Program	Description	Authors	Publisher
	Parenting, both based on the same model of self-determination, are available from the Center for Self-Determination and Transition at Wayne State University, e-mail: sdtalk@wayne.edu.) *Steps to Self-Determination* is experientially based, allowing students to establish and work toward goals as they acquire knowledge and skills listed in the model. The curriculum was designed to be used with students with and without disabilities and in a variety of scheduling arrangements.		
Social Stories and Songs for Children	Geared toward preschool and early elementary students. This group conducted research in early childhood settings to determine which self-determination skills were most pertinent to this age group. They found that the self-determination skills of solving problems, managing behavior, and sharing and following instructions were most appropriate to target for this range. *Social Stories and Songs for Children* focuses on teaching these concepts through stories, songs, and art activities.	Serna, Nielsen, & Forness (in press)	Research Press Champaign, IL http://www .researchpress.com

to participate in setting their own goals, if this is not possible and goals need to be set by teachers, then the student's preferences and interests should be incorporated into the goals to increase the student's motivation to pursue the goal. Goals that have personal meaning are more likely to be attained (Doll & Sands, 1998; Locke & Latham, 1990).

As we've noted, the educational planning process is an excellent context within which to teach goal setting. With regard to this, students can be taught the following:

1. Goals and objectives should be written to achieve outcomes that are based on each student's unique interests, abilities, and needs.

2. Goals should be attainable.

3. Goals and objectives should be measurable.

4. Goals and objectives should have a starting time and an ending time.

5. Goals and objectives should be written in terms of expected outcomes.

Karvonen et al. (2004) did an in-depth study of several schools promoting self-determination. At three of the sites they visited, notable strategies to teach goal setting (other than through the Individualized Education Program [IEP] process) were observed. One of the sites had students develop personal goal statements and then decide whom they would recruit to help them reach their goals. Another school offered a transition course for which the students helped to establish the goals. Yet another class elected officers who met weekly to plan the class activities for the following week. This class was cotaught by faculty members who had responsibility for designing instruction to meet the goals set by the students.

Eisenman and Chamberlin (2001) found that creating self-directed learning environments promoted goal setting and attainment. Staff in these schools found that "students who are taught and supported to take responsibility for setting learning goals, monitoring their progress, and managing the quality of the learning environment would be developing attributes of self-determined individuals" (p. 144). By helping students learn to set and work toward goals in the context of their academic instruction, teachers in these schools found that they were able to help students learn important skills for self-determination while increasing the likelihood of improved academic achievement.

Another way that goal setting (along with choice making, independent performance, and planning and evaluation) was promoted by one school in Eisenman and Chamberlin's (2001) study was through school-based enterprise. The school offered a series of classes in printing. The students operated and managed all aspects of a printing business as they moved through their course work. Goal setting was one of the key skills they needed to learn and practice in order to run the school-based business.

Teaching Problem Solving

A number of strategies to promote problem solving have been evaluated for students with disabilities. Bauminger (2002) developed a curriculum to teach students with autism social and interpersonal problem-solving skills. Students were taught about social concepts, such as starting a conversation, and then were presented a vignette of a student having difficulty implementing the skill. Students went through an eight-stage problem-solving process with their teacher:

1. Define the problem.

2. Discuss the emotions associated with the problem.

3. Define the alternative social actions.

4. Consider the consequences of each alternative.

5. Make a decision about the best alternative.

6. Role-play the solution with their teacher.

7. Receive homework to practice the social skill covered in the lesson at home with peers.

8. Receive feedback from the teacher on the homework.

After seven months, students generated more appropriate solutions to problems faced in social situations and initiated more social interactions with their peers. Form 5.1 provides a template students can use to implement the key problem-solving steps.

Bernard-Opitz, Sriram, and Nakhoda-Sapuan (2001) developed a computer program to teach students with developmental disabilities social problem-solving skills. The program first presented pictures or videos of people experiencing social conflicts. The program guided students through an animated problem-solving process, in which they were asked to generate alternative solutions. After identifying an alternate solution, a video clip of the actors resolving the problem was presented. As students had repeated experience with the program, they generated more alternative solutions. The increase in the generation of solutions observed in this study and in the Bauminger (2002) study is important, as research suggests that generating more solutions to a problem often leads to a better resolution (D'Zurilla & Nezu, 1980).

Teaching Decision Making

Instruction to enable students to learn how to make effective decisions can be infused into school counseling programs, academic classes

Form 5.1   A Problem-Solving Guide

1. What is your problem? _____

   _____

   Have you written your problem so that you can see how to solve it?   Yes   No

2. How does this problem make you feel? _____

   _____

3. What options are available to solve the problem?

   a. _____

   b. _____

   c. _____

   d. _____

4. What will happen if you implement each option?

   a. _____

   b. _____

   c. _____

   d. _____

5. Which option is best to solve the problem? _____

   _____

(e.g., language arts, social studies, creative writing), academic support classes (e.g., resource rooms, study skills), career preparation classes, and extracurricular activities. Such instruction should not be an "add-on." Rather, it should be infused throughout the school day so that students are able to see the practical application of the instruction.

To support students in their acquisition of decision-making skills, a number of strategies can be implemented throughout the student's educational career. Early on, students should be provided with a wide array of choice opportunities, as discussed previously, and receive instruction regarding how to make effective choices. As students age, they should be provided overt instruction in the decision-making process. A number of curricular approaches have been developed to promote decision-making skills (see Baron & Brown, 1991), all of which can be individualized based on a student's learning and support needs. Opportunities for students to make decisions should be embedded in the curriculum. By supporting students to make decisions in real-world situations, they will further develop their ability to conceptualize and generalize the decision-making process.

There are several frameworks available to define the steps in decision making. Two of these frameworks are provided in Table 5.2. As with choice making, students need direct instruction and guided practice in these steps if they are going to learn to make good decisions. It is important to note that we define good decisions as those that help students obtain the outcomes they deem most important to them, those that reflect a sense of self-determination.

It is typically best to help students learn to make decisions about issues that have the potential for fewer negative consequences first and then move on to those decisions that are likely to have a stronger impact on their lives. For example, students could begin to learn about the decision-making process by making decisions about a book they would like to read, a movie they would like to see, the manner in which they would like to complete an assignment, or a leisure activity they would like to try. (Note: To teach decision making, rather than the related area of choice making, it is important that the student generates the options to choose from rather than someone else providing them with the options.) As they have become more proficient and confident in their choice making, students can move on to making bigger decisions, with greater consequences, such as jobs they would like to try out, courses they would like to take, or careers they might like to pursue.

Fostering Self-Awareness and Self-Knowledge

If students are to act in a self-determined manner, they must possess a basic understanding of their individual strengths, abilities, limitations, and

Table 5.2 Decision-Making Frameworks

Janis and Mann (1977)

1. Consider a wide range of alternative courses of action.
2. Survey the full range of objectives to be fulfilled and values implicated by the choice.
3. Carefully weigh the positive and negative consequences of each alternative.
4. Intensely search for new information and evaluate alternatives.
5. Correctly assimilate new information.
6. Reexamine positive and negative consequences of alternatives.
7. Detail provisions for implementing chosen alternatives.

Hogarth (1980)

1. Structure the problem.
2. Assess consequences.
3. Assess uncertainties.
4. Evaluate alternatives.
5. Analyze sensitively.
6. Gather information.
7. Choose.

---

unique learning needs, and they must know how to use these unique attributes to enhance their quality of life. The development of both self-awareness and self-knowledge requires the acquisition of a categorical sense of self, that is, an understanding of one's uniqueness and separateness from others. This typically occurs early in child development. In subsequent years, self-awareness and self-knowledge require an accurate sense of the cognitive self or an understanding of one's own thinking and reasoning acts, as well as the capacity to deliberately manipulate these to suit one's purposes.

Self-awareness is built through our interaction with the environment, including the messages we hear from other people, and from listening to our own internal voice through our emotional and cognitive reactions to experiences. Therefore, providing students with a range of experiences and support for understanding what their experiences mean in terms of their preferences, interests, values, strengths, and weaknesses is an important instructional component of self-determination.

Career exploration programs can be an excellent vehicle to help older students develop increased self-awareness and self-knowledge. Eisenman and Chamberlin (2001) reported on the results of a cluster evaluation of self-determination activities for several schools within a state. They found that participating schools often promoted the self-determination components of self-awareness and goal setting through existing career awareness and exploration activities. Eisenman and Chamberlin reported on one vocational-technical school where students participated in a coordinated sequence of career exploration activities that culminated in a co-op placement in the senior year. As part of this program, a special education job coach implemented a variety of self-awareness and goal-setting activities with students, with and without disabilities, beginning in the freshman year. In another school, self-awareness was promoted through the career exploration program by offering a ninth-grade exploratory course that addressed all of the career pathways offered in the school. Part of examining the career pathways included helping students to explore their preferences, interests, strengths, and weaknesses in relation to each of the career pathways. Other ways in which schools reported that their career preparation program promoted self-awareness was through the use of career exploration activities via a career decision-making software program and participation in activities sponsored by the business-industry-education alliance (BIE). The BIE sponsored activities such as career presentations, job site visitations, and development of career portfolios.

One of the schools in Eisenman and Chamberlin's (2001) evaluation provided support for increased self-awareness by infusing lessons from the Life Centered Career Education (LCCE; Brolin, 1997) curriculum into their instruction. They selected lessons from LCCE that were most directly related to self-determination and self-awareness (Wehmeyer, 1995). They implemented approximately 20 of the LCCE lessons from the personal/social skills domain, achieving self-awareness competency. The LCCE lessons included having students identify physical and psychological needs, personal interests, and abilities.

Too frequently the only time the issue of student self-awareness comes to the forefront in education is when persons other than the student question the degree to which he or she has "accepted" his or her disability or, in less positive terms, accepts what he or she cannot do because of the disability. When self-awareness is seen only in terms of students accepting what they cannot do, the course of treatment is too often "forcing" students to "accept" their disability. While disability awareness is an important part of self-awareness, understanding one's disability and its effects on how one interacts with the environment and other people should not be the goal of educational efforts to promote self-awareness. Instead, such efforts should be focused on promoting student self-acceptance through self-understanding and self-knowledge and on enabling students to use their unique skills and abilities to their greatest advantage.

It is important to promote *realistic* self-awareness and self-knowledge in students with disabilities. For example, Faherty (2000) developed an approach to guide children and youth with autism spectrum disorders through the process of developing an understanding of their strengths, their abilities, and the impact of autism on their lives. The process has a number of activities that encourage students to think about their strengths and abilities, and it contains activities to support students to develop and reflect on how they learn, their sensory experiences, their artistic and technological abilities, their social and communication skills, their thoughts, and why they sometimes feel upset. It also helps students reflect on the people in their lives, including their school experiences.

Promoting Choice Making

Providing students with appropriate opportunities to learn choice-making skills is an important strategy for helping students acquire and apply skills and knowledge related to self-determination (Field & Hoffman, 2002b; Lehmann, 1993). Abery (1994, p. 355) described the choice-making process by delineating eight major steps:

1. An awareness of preferences

2. An appreciation that choices among preferences are possible

3. Recognition of decision-making opportunities

4. Definition of the choice or decision at hand

5. Setting of personal outcome standards

6. Generation of alternative choices

7. Evaluation of alternatives

8. Selection of the alternative that most closely meets the individual's goals

Students need to be provided with instruction and support for learning the steps in making choices. They need to be instructed and guided through the eight steps delineated above. Many teachers have found it useful to guide a group of students through the choice-making process for a group decision first and then help students apply the choice-making steps on an individual basis.

As we are helping students learn about making choices, it is imperative that we give students the opportunity to learn by doing. Safety nets must be built into the process, so that students have the opportunity to recover if they make a choice that has negative consequences. Failure is a learning experience only if it is followed by success. We need to help students learn how to recover from the consequences of choices they don't like if we are going to help them to stay motivated to take a risk again. This is especially important in the early stages of learning about choice making. Therefore, when we are designing activities to help children and youth learn to make choices, it is helpful to predict ways students might recover from making a bad choice.

Providing students with opportunities to make choices in school allows them to receive, apply, and practice feedback on their choice-making skills in a safe setting. Providing students with opportunities for choice allows them to learn as they experience the natural consequences of their decisions in real environments. If opportunities for choice are not provided, students may see little benefit in developing self-determination skills, or they may lose existing self-determination skills.

Attribution Retraining

Attributions are the assignments one makes about the cause of one's success or failure at various tasks. Adelman and Taylor (1993) described the tendency for "observers" (people in charge) to attribute behaviors to consistent personal dispositions and for "actors" (those being observed, such as students or employees) to attribute their actions to environmental factors. In contrast, students with disabilities often experience sufficient failure to expect it to continue, resulting in devastating effects on their self-esteem, willingness to take risks, and motivation about school (Smith, 1989). They come to attribute their failures to a lack of ability (internalizing the negative labels that the environment communicates) and to attribute their successes to luck, the ease of the task, or the fact that someone else gave them the answers (an external cause). Researchers have found that attributions can be changed, and students can be helped to understand the consequences of their active roles in the learning process. Smith outlined several facets of the retraining strategy, including

1. Encouraging task-specificity, with discussions focused on actual performance and how to improve it

2. Teaching learning and academic strategies and reinforcing students for using them

3. Encouraging students to task-analyze their learning tasks

4. Instructing students in self-management procedures

5. Discussing the knowledge, skills, and supports that contribute to students' achievements

Lovitt (1989) also offered several guidelines for, and empirical findings from, attribution retraining and stressed the importance of linking it with learning strategy and academic instruction.

In *The Optimistic Child* (1995), Martin Seligman outlined a process and several activities that teachers and parents can use to help children develop an optimistic explanatory style. A hallmark of an optimistic explanatory style is believing we can make positive things happen in our lives. Optimistic explanatory style is closely linked to having an internal locus of control and making (and believing) positive attributions about our abilities. Seligman outlined a process to help children and youth develop a more optimistic explanatory style by helping them learn about fundamentals of optimism through reading and responding to vignettes and by learning the skills of disputing and decatastrophizing to deal with negative self-talk. Seligman's recommendations for teachers and parents to help children and youth challenge their pessimistic beliefs and find a more accurate understanding of the causes of their setbacks are based in principles of cognitive therapy, which has been found to be highly successful in increasing locus of control and combating depression.

Curricular Materials

As mentioned above and identified in Table 5.1, several curricula have been designed specfically to help students develop greater proficiency in competencies related to self-determination. Most teachers have used these curricula in combination with existing academic content and teacher-designed instruction to help students acquire knowledge and skills for self-determination. Some of the curricula are focused specifically on the IEP process (see Table 3.3), and others are more general in nature (see Table 5.1). Some examples of widely used curricula to teach specific skills related to self-determination include the *ChoiceMaker* materials (Martin & Marshall, 1995), *Steps to Self-Determination* (Field & Hoffman, 1996; Hoffman & Field, 2006), and *Social Stories and Songs for Children* (Serna et al., in press). Table 5.3 provides the primary curricular areas addressed by the *ChoiceMaker* materials, while Table 5.4 provides the lesson themes for the *Steps to Self-Determination* curriculum.

Reviews and further information on these materials and several others are available at the University of North Carolina–Charlotte Web site for the Self-Determination Synthesis Project at http://www.uncc.edu/ sdsp or in *A Practical Guide to Teaching Self-Determination* (Field, Martin, Miller, Ward, & Wehmeyer, 1998).

Table 5.3   ChoiceMaker Self-Determination Transition Curriculum Sections, Goals, and Lessons

Section	Goals	Lessons
1. Choosing Goals	A. Student Interests B. Student Skills and Limits C. Student Goals	• Choosing Employment Goals • Choosing Personal Goals • Choosing Post–High School Goals • Choosing Secondary School Goals • Choosing Housing and Daily Living Goals • Choosing Community Participation Goals
2. Expressing Goals	D. Student Leading Meeting E. Student Reporting	• Self-Directed Individualized Education Program
3. Taking Action	F. Student Plan G. Student Action H. Student Evaluation I. Student Adjustment	• Take Action

SOURCE: Adapted from Martin, J. E., & Marshall, L. H. (1995). *ChoiceMaker self-determination instructional package.* Longmont, CO: Sopris West.

Table 5.4   Lesson Themes for Steps to Self-Determination

Session	Theme
1	Dreaming to Open Possibilities
2	What Is Important to Me?
3	Creating Options for Long-Term Goals
4	Setting Goals
5	Choosing Short-Term Goals
6	Planning the Steps to Reach Short-Term Goals
7	Planning Actions for the Steps
8	Taking the First Step
9	Creative Barrier Breaking
10	A Little Help From My Friends
11	A Journey to Self-Determination
12	Assertive Communication I
13	Assertive Communication II
14	Negotiation
15	Conflict Resolution
16	Where Do We Go From Here?

SOURCE: Adapted from Field, S., & Hoffman, A. (1996). *Steps to self-determination.* Austin, TX: PRO-ED.

Student-Directed Learning and Peer-Mediated Instructional Strategies

I n Chapter 5, we introduced key instructional activities, strategies, and methods teachers can use to promote self-determination. While goal setting, choice making, problem solving, and decision making are involved in enabling students to self-regulate their behavior and their lives, in this chapter, we overview student-directed learning strategies that do so directly. Next, we overview the Self-Determined Learning Model of Instruction, an instructional model designed to enable teachers to teach students, in essence, to teach themselves. Finally, we discuss peer-mediated strategies that can contribute to enhanced self-determination.

STUDENT-DIRECTED LEARNING STRATEGIES

Student-directed learning strategies involve teaching students strategies that enable them to modify and regulate their own behavior (Agran et al., 2003). These strategies, which include antecedent cue regulation, self-monitoring, self-instruction, self-evaluation, and self-reinforcement, are sometimes referred to as self-regulation strategies or self-management strategies. Self-regulated learning refers to "learning that occurs largely from the influence of students' self-generated thoughts, feelings, strategies, and behaviors, which are oriented toward the attainment of goals" (Schunk & Zimmerman, 1998, p. vii). More behaviorally oriented practitioners and researchers use the term *self-management,* referring, in general, to any responses or processes that enable a person to regulate or change his or her own behavior, though the strategies described as self-management or self-regulation strategies are almost identical. We prefer the term *student-directed learning strategies* because it emphasizes that the primary impetus for teaching and learning is on the student, and we use it as an umbrella term to cover self-regulation, self-management, and self-control strategies.

Meichenbaum and Biemiller (1998) summarized differences they had seen between "self-directed" and "other-directed" students:

In contrast to the less self-directed students, the highly self-directed students can accomplish academic tasks more successfully, and can explain their performance to others. They assume a higher level of responsibility for task accomplishment and achieve a higher level of mastery. (p. 57)

Research has consistently shown that students with disabilities can learn, implement, and benefit from these strategies. (See Agran et al., 2003, for a focus on students with severe disabilities; Reid, 1996, for a review with students with learning disabilities; Graham & Harris, 2005, for a focus on teaching writing; Pressley, 2005, for a focus on teaching reading; and Baumeister & Vohs, 2004, for a comprehensive review of self-regulation theory and practice.)

Antecedent Cue Regulation

We begin our overview of student-directed learning strategies at the beginning, as it were, with antecedent cue regulation strategies. The principles of applied behavior analysis have been applied to the design of a number of instructional techniques and strategies that are critical to the successful self-direction of students with disabilities, including antecedent cue regulation strategies. This type of strategy is based on the "three term contingency" outlined by applied behavior analysis. This refers to the three components of a behavioral action: the discriminative stimulus, the response, and the reinforcer or consequence. The discriminative stimulus is a specific event or environmental condition that serves as the "stimulus" to bring out the desired response. This stimulus is said to "acquire control" over the desired response when the response is paired with a reinforcer.

A common discriminative stimulus is a teacher instruction or prompt to perform a task. The response is the behavior the student performs when presented the discriminative stimulus. This is, in essence, the behavior you are trying to teach the student. The reinforcer, or reinforcing stimulus, is an event or action that follows the response and, importantly, increases the possibility that the response will be exhibited again.

Antecedent cue regulation strategies teach students to use behaviors that serve as the discriminative stimulus, to elicit or prompt the desired response or behavior. This sounds more complex than it really is. A common such strategy involves picture prompts (although we don't use the term *picture prompts* as the description for all such strategies because, simply, not all antecedent cue regulation strategies involve visual or picture prompts), and we'll describe picture prompting in some depth as a means to explain the overall purpose of antecedent cue regulation strategies.

Picture Prompting Strategies

Picture prompting strategies involve the use of visual prompts, which can be as simple as a line drawing or as sophisticated as a digital photograph. Students learn to use these pictures as visual cues that prompt them to perform a particular response. Such strategies are used mostly by students who are not able to use verbal or other cue systems, including students with mental retardation, autism, or traumatic brain injury. But anyone who has purchased a computer system recently has used a picture prompting strategy to assemble that computer, as most such systems come with instructions that are depicted in pictures or large drawings and provide step-by-step visual cues to assemble the computer, showing that picture prompting strategies can be used with a wider array of students.

In Chapter 2, we mentioned the potential role of technology in promoting self-determination, and this is a good point to show how technology can be used to promote self-determination by promoting student self-direction of learning. There are a growing number of digital or visual prompting systems available that run on software loaded on to portable or handheld computers, called PDAs (portable digital assistants). These PDA systems are just technologically sophisticated picture prompts. For example, one such system, called Visual Assistant (http://www.ablelink tech.com/), allows digital photographs of the steps in a task to be synchronized from a desktop computer to the PDA and then enables teachers, parents, and even the student to record audio messages associated with each picture, using the recording capabilities of the PDA itself. When a student wants to begin a task, he or she opens the Visual Assistant program on the PDA, taps the screen on a digital photo of the task itself to open the particular task, and then taps a "Start" button on the screen to begin the program. The digital picture of the first step in the task is loaded, and the audio message describing what the student is supposed to do is played. When the student completes that step of the task, he or she taps on a "Done" button on the screen, which then brings up the next step in the task, plays the audio message, and so on. Our own research with the Visual Assistant (Davies, Stock, & Wehmeyer, 2002; Riffel et al., 2005) has shown that students with intellectual disabilities can decrease their dependence on external prompts and perform transition-related tasks more independently. These PDA-based visual prompting systems could, however, be equally applicable across multiple academic or functional tasks and across students with and without disabilities as can be the general strategy of picture or audio prompting systems. For example, Brown, Ilderton, and Taylor (2001) recommended using picture prompts to support students with attention problems in the classroom by placing pictures on the student's desk to remind him or her of appropriate ways to attend or participate in class activities.

Designing Antecedent Cue Regulation Strategies

Agran et al. (2003) identified several steps to designing an antecedent cue regulation system:

1. Select a target task. Tasks that lend themselves to these types of strategies are those for which there are a sequence of steps the student must learn or perform and, often, for which students currently depend on others for prompting to engage in one or more steps.

2. Break the task into steps. This is simply the process of task analysis. In task analysis, you break a task or activity into its component steps. A task analysis is simply identifying the steps that, when chained together, form the steps required to perform a skill or activity. Table 6.1 provides suggested steps for conducting a task analysis.

3. Select a type of prompt. Is it best to use a visual prompt, an audio prompt, or both, as with the Visual Assistant? This can be a function of the student's learning preferences but can also depend on the context. In some situations, having an audio prompt would be disruptive. What types of visual or audio prompts seem best?

4. Create a prompt for each step.

Table 6.1   Steps to Task Analysis

Step	Actions
Define the target skill or task.	
Identify the constituent steps in the activity.	• Perform the task yourself. • Observe other students performing the task.
Write down the task or activity steps.	• State the task in terms of observable behavior. • Order the steps according to their place in the actual sequence. • Write the task in first-person singular (I) for use with self-directed audio prompts.
Determine if any of the steps can or need to be broken down any further.	
Determine what steps need to be incorporated into picture or audio prompt.	• Observe target student.

5. Decide how the prompt will be delivered. Will you use a PDA or put pictures in a small photo album as the delivery mechanism? Will you use a tape recorder? Again, the context can make a difference. If the student needs to leave the prompting system in one location, a less expensive (and less prone to be stolen) photo album may be best.

Just remember, *antecedent* means "before," and antecedent cue regulation strategies simply teach students ways to prompt themselves before they perform a step in a task, using whatever means works best.

Self-Monitoring, Self-Evaluation, and Self-Reinforcement

Self-monitoring is, basically, the data collection phase of student self-directed learning and can and should be incorporated into instruction throughout the student's instructional day. Self-evaluation involves taking the data collected through self-monitoring and making a judgment as to progress toward a goal. Self-reinforcement involves teaching students to provide their own reinforcement when completing a task. Because the three strategies are closely linked, we will discuss them here together.

Teaching students to self-monitor involves a two-step process. First, students must learn to discriminate when they have successfully completed a step, task, or action; or have engaged in a behavior or action to a predetermined level of accuracy, mastery, or duration; or, alternatively, have refrained from engaging in a behavior or action for a predetermined duration. Second, they must learn how to accurately record that fact. Self-monitoring is pretty much that simple: Teach students to discriminate when they've done something well and teach them to record that fact.

There are numerous advantages to teaching students to self-monitor their behavior. Daly and Ranalli (2003) noted that teaching students to self-monitor benefits the student in that it (a) provides a clearer picture to students of their own behavior or progress, (b) provides immediate feedback to students, (c) facilitates communication with parents by enabling students to report their progress, and (d) facilitates cooperative interactions among students because it is a within-student and not a between-student comparison. Teacher benefits include ease of use, inexpensiveness of implementation, enhanced student independence, enhanced student generalization, and adaptation across settings (Schloss & Smith, 1998).

Teaching Self-Monitoring

The first step in teaching self-monitoring is to teach the student to discriminate when he or she has correctly completed a task. Schloss and Smith (1998) suggested several steps to teaching self-monitoring:

1. Clearly define the behavior that will be self-monitored. One key to successful self-monitoring is to ensure that students can clearly identify when they have completed a particular step, target, or goal. Much as is the case for many other applied behavior analytic strategies, clearly defining the target behavior in observable, measurable terms is essential. If the student is monitoring the target to "do good work," it is quite likely that the ambiguity of "good" will diminish the probability that students will accurately record progress and, as such, will impact, if not erase, the benefit of self-monitoring.

2. Explain the purpose of self-monitoring. Student-directed learning strategies must, by definition, be transparent to students. That is, they need to be aware of what the strategy is, how it is used, what it can help them achieve, and how to implement it. Further, one of the benefits of self-monitoring is that the action of recording progress on a goal serves, to some degree, as a discriminative stimulus—a cue, as it were, for performing the behavior again, but only if students are conscious of using the strategy.

3. Model the self-monitoring strategy. One of the benefits of self-monitoring is that such procedures can be designed to fit any task for any student, a fact we will return to momentarily. Whatever self-monitoring

process is identified or created, however, it is important to teach the student to use it correctly, and that will start with modeling how the process itself works, including both how to use the self-monitoring process and when to self-monitor.

4. Practice with role playing. Provide examples of appropriate and inappropriate times to self-monitor. You can also let students practice with the process before they actually implement it, though you must be sure to monitor their performance to make sure they're using it correctly.

Types of Data

Just as when you are collecting data on student performance yourself, there are many types of data collection procedures that can be used in the context of self-monitoring. These include frequency counts (e.g., counting the actual number of occurrences of a correct response); duration (a length of time over which a response or behavior occurs or doesn't occur); type, level, or frequency of prompt needed; and so forth. All of these can be used in self-monitoring. For example, for an academic goal related to completing a predetermined number of whole number division problems, a logical approach would be to have the student record the frequency of correct problems or, perhaps, the frequency of worksheets with a certain percentage correct. If, on the other hand, the goal is to have a student refrain from speaking during certain class periods, it might be best to have students record how long they behave appropriately or, mixing the two, recording the frequency of five-minute intervals in which the student does not speak out.

Self-Monitoring Across Content Areas

As we've noted, self-monitoring can be applied to multiple content areas, and the types of data collected will vary according to content areas. For example, Graham and Harris (2005, p. 45) suggested a three-step self-monitoring process for writing output that involves the use of frequency data:

1. After they have completed their writing, students count all the words in the composition, including title.

2. Students then record the total number of words in their composition in a bar graph or a graphing paper sheet.

3. After each recording, students compare their output with previous such outputs. (This is, in essence, a self-evaluation step, which will be discussed subsequently.)

Graham and Harris (2005) suggest three tips to improve student performance when using this self-monitoring process. First, you may need to help younger children count and chart. Second, you can improve performance by linking goal-setting activities to the self-monitoring process. Using several self-monitoring sessions as baseline data, have students set a goal pertaining to the number of words they would like to eventually write in a composition. Finally, this strategy focuses on the length of the composition, but you may be equally concerned with the quality of the writing, so teacher evaluation of product quality should accompany the self-monitoring data. In addition to self-monitoring for word output, Graham and Harris have shown the efficacy of self-monitoring for story parts (monitoring the inclusion of basic parts or elements of a story), use of action, description or transition words, and types of revisions made.

Similarly, Jitendra et al. (2000) used self-monitoring to improve reading comprehension for students with learning and behavioral disorders. The primary intervention to improve text comprehension was teaching main idea comprehension. Self-monitoring was used to check the students' use of this strategy. Students used a self-monitoring card on which four primary tasks in reading comprehension were listed: (1) Read the paragraph, (2) use a prompt card to prompt the use of the main idea strategy, (3) use the main idea strategy, and (4) select or write the main idea (Jitendra et al., 2000, p. 131). Students showed marked improvement in reading comprehension maintained over time.

Finally, self-monitoring can be used with a host of nonacademic content areas, including teaching social skills, vocational and transition skills, and virtually any other skill. For example, Daly and Ranalli (2003) used a device called "countoons" to teach self-monitoring of appropriate behavior to students with emotional and behavioral disabilities. Countoons are cartoon representations of appropriate and inappropriate behavior. We've created a sample countoon in Figure 6.1. As you can see, countoons typically have four frames, much like a cartoon strip in a newspaper. Frames one and three depict students engaged in appropriate behavior. In our sample, this involves bringing both paper and pencil to class. Daly and Ranalli modified the original countoon sequence and had the second frame depict the student engaged in an inappropriate behavior and the fourth frame showing the consequence or reward associated with engaging in appropriate behavior. In Figure 6.1, the inappropriate behavior is bringing only paper, and the reward is time playing a video game. Above the second (inappropriate behavior) and below the third (appropriate behavior) frames are squares with numbers that allow students to count, or self-monitor, their inappropriate or appropriate behavior.

Figure 6.1   Sample Countoon

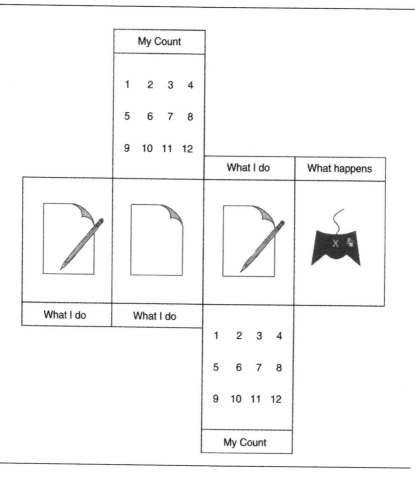

Types of Behavior to Self-Monitor

We have indicated that self-monitoring can be applied to virtually any content area. There are, however, three general types of self-monitoring that refer more to the type of behavior being monitored rather than the specific content (e.g., math, reading, social skills). These are self-monitoring of performance, self-monitoring of attention, and self-monitoring of strategy use (Harris, Friedlander, Saddler, Frizzelle, & Graham, 2005).

Self-monitoring of performance. This involves recording and monitoring student performance of the task being monitored, is typically associated with academic tasks, and includes data on frequency correct and percentage correct or attempted.

Self-monitoring of attention. This involves collecting data on factors such as time on task, time spent, and other attentional behaviors. This type frequently involves duration data.

Self-monitoring of strategy use. This type involves the use of frequency counts, typically, to record the use of a particular strategy, such as that used in the Jitendra et al. (2000) study described previously.

Recording Forms for Self-Monitoring

Perhaps the area that can make this strategy most useful for a wide array of students involves the particular recording form or format selected. The most commonly used recording format is a self-monitoring card or graph sheet, on which the student simply writes his or her self-monitored data. The type of data might dictate certain formats. If students are to record the occurrence of a behavior anytime it occurs, then having boxes to check off makes sense. If students are to record the performance of a set of actions, such as in self-monitoring of strategy use, then a list of the strategies is helpful. If students are doing frequency counts, then having graph paper onto which they can chart and immediately bar graph their frequencies takes away the need to summarize the data later on.

Similarly, all word processing programs have fully functional charting and graphing features, and it would be quite simple to establish a database into which students could enter data that would then be graphed or charted automatically. Software programs like Microsoft Excel are fairly simple to use, and some students can use an Excel spreadsheet for their data entry and display.

Many students with cognitive disabilities and young children, however, will not be able to use even simply written or graphing types of formats. Does this mean that they cannot self-monitor their behavior? Of course not; it just means that you have to be more creative in designing a monitoring format. So, for example, giving a student some marbles and a jar with a line drawn three quarters up the jar can be a simple-to-use format. The student can be taught to put one marble in the jar for each time they successfully perform the task. When the marbles reach the line, the student has reached his or her goal.

Teaching Self-Evaluation

Self-monitoring is useful because it can serve as a cue to students pertaining to appropriate or successful behavior. The primary purpose, however, of collecting such data is to use the data to evaluate performance and to track progress toward a goal. Self-evaluation involves teaching students to compare his or her behavior or performance with some standard or criteria typically specified by a goal. The self-evaluation process typically uses data from the self-monitoring process to evaluate the student's progress toward his or her goal. This can be as complex or as simple as it needs to be. In the case of the marble-in-the-jar example, the goal might be to fill the jar up to the line, and the self-evaluation process might involve simply asking the student if there are marbles all the way to the line. In other cases, though, filling the jar to the line might just be the first point at which the student would receive reinforcement for his or her progress, and the goal might be to fill the jar 10 times. In the case of the self-monitoring for the writing output strategy we discussed earlier, students may set a goal to have 150 words in a composition for five consecutive sessions. The self-evaluation process would involve looking at the bar graph to track and determine when that goal has been reached.

Self-evaluation procedures can also be used without an associated self-monitoring process. In this case, teachers typically set up some sort of rubric that students can use to evaluate their behavior or performance. Such rubrics are typically in a Likert-type format (e.g., 1 = excellent work, 2 = good work, 3 = satisfactory work, 4 = less than satisfactory work, and 5 = poor work) and can be accompanied by visual representations for younger students or students with cognitive disabilities.

Like self-monitoring, though, self-evaluation strategies have to be taught. Agran et al. (2003, pp. 71–74) suggested several steps to teaching self-evaluation:

1. Make sure the student knows the targeted behavior or performance level and provide examples and non-examples of this.

2. Emphasize the benefits of the desired or targeted behavior, much as the countoons provide information about the consequence.

3. Teach students the self-evaluation process.

4. Model the self-evaluation process.

5. Provide guided practice using the self-evaluation process.

6. Provide independent practice opportunities to self-assess.

7. Verify student mastery of the self-evaluation process.

Teaching Self-Reinforcement

Teaching students to provide reinforcement for appropriate behaviors or successful performances involves many of the same steps associated with teaching self-evaluation, with a focus on when the student can self-reinforce.

This may be at the end of a class period or the school day, but it might also be at the start of the day, depending on the nature of the task. For example, if the task involves arriving to the first class of the day on time, the self-reinforcement should be immediately after that. At other times, it is linked to goal attainment and, as such, can be incorporated as the final step of the self-evaluation process.

Self-Instruction

The final student-directed learning strategy we'll cover is self-instruction. When students are taught to self-instruct, they learn to use their own verbal behavior to guide their performance (Hughes & Agran, 1993). Self-instruction is a critical student-directed learning strategy that contributes to a student's self-determination. Like self-monitoring, self-instruction statements can serve as instructional cues or prompts that increase the probability that the targeted behavior will be performed. Self-instruction also may serve as a self-regulation strategy in which language mediates behavior.

In a general sense, self-instruction simply refers to a process in which a person tells himself or herself to do something, and then does it. Meichenbaum and Goodman (1971) developed a sequence for teaching self-instruction that has become the prototype for many teaching applications. Their sequence consisted of five steps, including (1) teacher performs task, instructing aloud while student observes, (2) student performs task while teacher instructs aloud, (3) student performs task while self-instructing aloud, (4) student performs task while whispering, and (5) student performs task while self-instructing "covertly."

Teachers may choose from several models of self-instruction when teaching students to guide their own behavior. The traditional teaching model is based on Meichenbaum and Goodman's (1971) original sequence and comprises four basic steps: (1) stating a problem, (2) stating a possible response to the problem, (3) evaluating the response, and (4) verbally reinforcing oneself.

Agran and colleagues (2003) identified a number of self-instruction models that have been validated with students with cognitive disabilities. These models include *Did-Next-Now, What/Where,* and *Interactive* self-instructional strategies, which may be adapted for students with mild or severe disabilities. *Did-Next-Now* is especially useful for teaching students to perform a series of tasks in a sequence. This model involves teaching a student to state the response just completed ("Did") and the next response to be performed ("Next"), and then to direct himself or herself to perform that response ("Now").

The *What/Where* self-instructional model is used to help guide a student's performance in response to an instruction. Students are taught to select key words from a verbal or written instruction and to determine *what* they are to do and *where* to do it. For students who have difficulty following instructions, the *What/Where* strategy provides them with a procedure to identify the relevant information in an instruction that will serve to guide their performance. The *Interactive* self-instructional model teaches students to state their self-instructions as questions that are embedded in conversation.

Like self-monitoring, self-instructional strategies have been shown to be effective across content areas, including academic, vocational/ transition, and social skills, as well as with students with a wide array of abilities. Wehmeyer, Agran, and Hughes (1998, pp. 177–180) made the following recommendations with regard to enhancing the impact of self-instruction:

1. The most reliable method for teachers to use in determining who will benefit from self-instructional training is to observe a student's preferences and responses. For example, does the student talk aloud? Does she repeat instructions heard? What words does she consistently use? While there are formats for nonverbal self-instruction, these communication abilities may be critical to success.

2. Teaching all four statements of Meichenbaum and Goodman's (1971) self-instructional teaching sequence (i.e., stating the problem, stating the response, self-evaluating, self-reinforcing) and asking learners to verbalize them consistently are recommended in order to produce generalization.

3. Teachers should be aware that the number of training sessions required to achieve proficiency in self-instructing may vary considerably across students. Teachers should establish a criterion for ending instruction based on a student's performance in both training and noninstructional settings. Instruction should be continued until a student has demonstrated clear mastery of self-instructional procedures and behavior change has been observed consistently in order to ensure that self-instruction will be maintained when instructional support is withdrawn.

4. Teachers should be flexible in allowing students who have limited verbal skills to self-instruct in nontraditional ways, including using sign language, pictures, or other symbolic means.

5. Teachers should use consistent, systematic direct instructional methods such as prompting, modeling, reinforcing, and providing corrective feedback when teaching students to self-instruct.

6. Active participation by a student in designing a self-instructional program may relate to the effectiveness of instruction.

7. Finally, teachers need to evaluate the effects of self-instructional training throughout their intervention efforts to determine if students actually are self-instructing and if self-instruction is correlated with desired behavior change.

Multiple Strategy Use

As we have indicated throughout this chapter, it is quite likely that you will want to combine these student-directed learning strategies to create intervention packages that implement all or some of them. One instructional model that does this, as well as integrating student-directed learning strategies with goal setting and problem solving, is the Self-Determined Learning Model of Instruction (Wehmeyer et al., 2000), which is described next.

The Self-Determined Learning Model of Instruction

Teaching students to self-direct their learning, to set goals, to solve problems, or to advocate for themselves often does not lend itself to traditional teaching models. Joyce and Weil (1980) defined a model of teaching as "a plan or pattern that can be used to shape curriculums (long term courses of study), to design instructional materials, and to guide instruction in the classroom and other settings" (p. 1). Such models are derived from theories about human behavior, learning, or cognition, and effective teachers employ multiple models of teaching, taking into account the unique characteristics of the learner and types of learning.

Like all educators, teachers working with students with disabilities use a variety of teaching models based on a student's learning characteristics and the content under consideration. A teacher may use the role-playing model to teach social behaviors, social simulation and social inquiry models to examine social problems and solutions, assertiveness training to teach self-advocacy skills, or a training model to teach vocational skills. Likewise, special educators employ more traditional, cognitively based models of teaching, such as the concept attainment model to teach thinking skills, the memory model for increasing the retention of facts, or inductive thinking and inquiry training models to teach reasoning and academic skills. The teaching model most frequently adopted by special educators is the contingency management model, drawing from principles contained in operant psychology.

The common theme across these models of teaching is that they are teacher directed. While they provide direction for strategy and curriculum development activities that can teach components of self-determination, none adequately provides teachers a model to truly enable young people to become causal agents in their lives. The Self-Determined Learning Model of Instruction (Wehmeyer et al., 2000) was developed to address this problem and is based on the component elements of self-determination, the process of self-regulated problem solving, and research on student-directed learning. It is appropriate for use with students with and without disabilities across a wide range of content areas and enables teachers to engage students in the totality of their educational program by increasing opportunities to self-direct learning and, in the process, to improve students' prospects for success after they leave school.

Implementation of the model consists of a three-phase instructional process depicted in Figures 6.2, 6.3, and 6.4. Each instructional phase presents a problem to be solved by the student. The student solves each problem by posing and answering a series of four student questions per phase that students learn, modify to make their own, and apply to reach self-selected goals. Each question is linked to a set of teacher objectives. Each instructional phase includes a list of educational supports that teachers can use to enable students to self-direct learning. In each instructional phase, the student is the primary agent for choices, decisions, and actions, even when eventual actions are teacher directed.

The student questions in the model are constructed to direct the student through a problem-solving sequence in each instructional phase. The solutions to the problems in each phase lead to the problem-solving sequence in the next phase. Their construction was based on theory in the problem-solving and self-regulation literature that suggests that there is a sequence of thoughts and actions, a means-end problem-solving sequence, that must be followed for any person's actions to produce results that satisfy their needs and interests. Teachers implementing the model teach students to solve a sequence of problems to construct a means-end chain—a causal sequence—that moves them from where they are (an actual state of not having their needs and interests satisfied) to where they want to be (a goal state of having those needs and interests satisfied). Its function is to reduce or eliminate the discrepancy between what students want or need and what students currently have or know. We construct this means-end sequence by having students answer the questions that connect their needs and interests to their actions and results via goals and plans.

Figure 6.2   Self-Determined Learning Model of Instruction: Phase 1

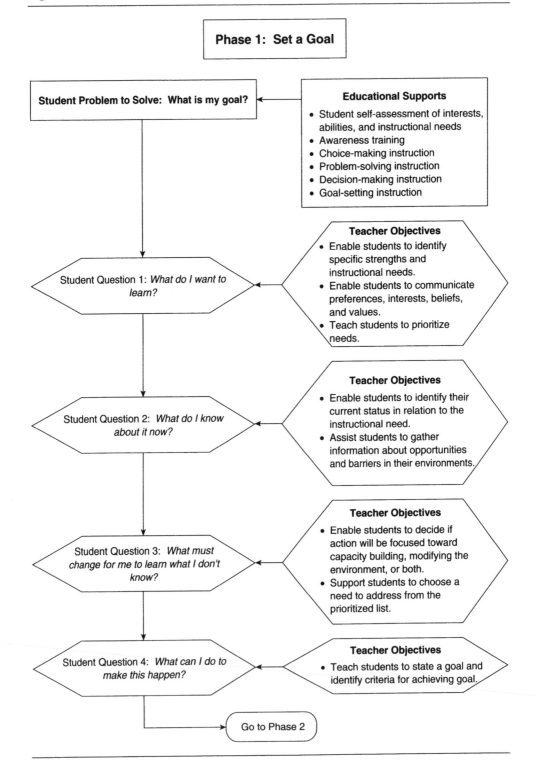

Figure 6.3 Self-Determined Learning Model of Instruction: Phase 2

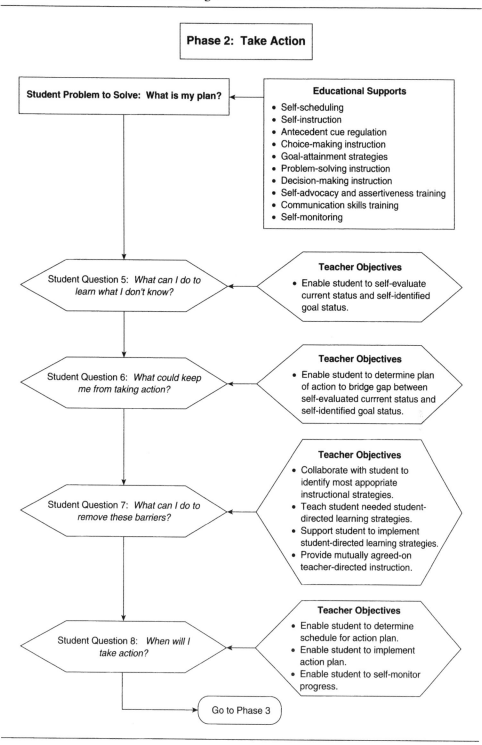

Figure 6.4   Self-Determined Learning Model of Instruction: Phase 3

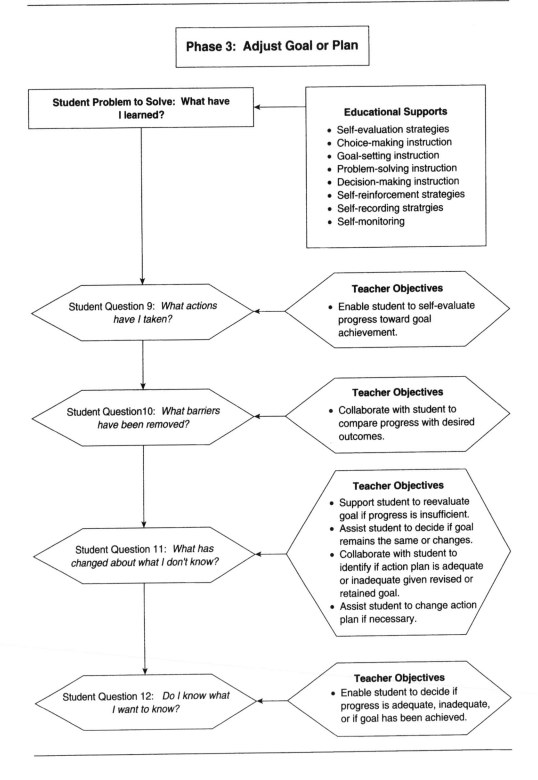

To answer the questions in this sequence, students must regulate their own problem solving by setting goals to meet needs, constructing plans to meet goals, and adjusting actions to complete plans. Thus each instructional phase poses a problem the student must solve (What is my goal? What is my plan? What have I learned?) by, in turn, solving a series of problems posed by the questions in each phase. The four questions differ from phase to phase but represent identical steps in the problem-solving sequence. That is, students answering the questions must (1) identify the problem, (2) identify potential solutions to the problem, (3) identify barriers to solving the problem, and (4) identify consequences of each solution. These steps are the fundamental steps in any problem-solving process, and they form the means-end problem-solving sequence represented by the student questions in each phase and enable the student to solve the problem posed in each instructional phase.

Because the model itself is designed for teachers to implement, the language of the student questions are, intentionally, not written to be understood by every student, nor does the model assume that students have life experiences that enable them to fully answer each question. The student questions are written in first-person voice in a relatively simple format with the intention that they are the starting point for discussion between the teacher and the student. Some students will learn and use all 12 questions as they are written. Other students will need to have the questions rephrased to be more easily understood. Still other students, due to the intensity of their instructional needs, may need to have the teacher paraphrase the questions for them.

The first time a teacher uses the model with a student, the initial step in the implementation process is to read the question with or to the student, discuss what the question means, and then, if necessary, change the wording to enable that student to better understand the intent of the question. Such wording changes, however, must be made such that the problem-solving intent of the question remains intact. For example, changing Student Question 1 from "What do I want to learn?" to "What is my goal?" changes the nature of the question. The teacher's objectives associated with each student question provide direction for possible wording changes. It is perhaps less important that actual changes in the words occur than that students take ownership over the process and adopt the question as their own, instead of having questions imposed on them. Going through this process once, as the student progresses through the model, should result in a set of questions that a student accepts as his or her own.

The teacher objectives within the model are just that—the objectives a teacher will be trying to accomplish by implementing the model. In each instructional phase, the objectives are linked directly to the student questions. These objectives can be met by utilizing strategies provided in the educational supports section of the model. The teacher objectives provide, in essence, a road map to assist the teacher to enable the student to solve the problem stated in the student question. For example, regarding Student Question 1: What do I want to learn?, teacher objectives linked to this question comprise the activities in which students should be engaged in order to answer this question. In this case, it involves enabling students to identify their specific strengths and instructional needs; to identify and communicate preferences, interests, beliefs, and values; and to prioritize their instructional needs. As teachers use the model, it is likely that they can generate more objectives that are relevant to the question, and they are encouraged to do so.

The educational supports are not actually a part of the model, per se, but are what Joyce and Weil (1980) refer to as the model's *syntax*—how the model is implemented. However, because the implementation of this model requires teachers to teach students to self-direct learning, we believe it is important to identify some strategies and supports that can be used to successfully implement the model. The majority of these supports are derived from the self-management literature, as discussed in the previous section.

The model's emphasis on the use of instructional strategies and educational supports that are student directed provides another means of teaching students to teach themselves. As we have already indicated, teaching students to use the student questions provided by the model will teach them a self-regulated problem-solving strategy. Concurrently, teaching students to use various student-directed learning strategies provides students with another layer of skills that enables them to become causal agents in their lives.

As important as it is to utilize the student-directed learning strategies, not every instructional strategy implemented will be student directed. The purpose of any model of teaching is to promote student learning and growth. There are circumstances in which the most effective instructional method or strategy to achieve a particular educational outcome will be a teacher-directed strategy. Students who are considering what plan of action to implement to achieve a self-selected goal can recognize that teachers have expertise in instructional strategies and take full advantage of that expertise.

The Self-Determined Learning Model of Instruction has been validated with students with disabilities, including students with learning disabilities, mental retardation, emotional and behavior disorders, and autism, as an effective means to promote student acquisition of educationally relevant goals (see Wehmeyer, Abery, Mithaug, & Stancliffe, 2003, for more detailed information).

PEER-MEDIATED LEARNING STRATEGIES

We discussed teacher-directed strategies to promote self-determination in Chapter 5 and have devoted most of this chapter to student-directed strategies. A third class of instructional strategies is peer-mediated learning strategies. Students with disabilities can learn a lot about being more self-determined simply by interacting with students without disabilities. Peers can be positive role models for goal setting, problem solving, and other component elements of self-determined behavior.

In addition, however, peers can become involved in efforts to promote the self-direction of learning by students with disabilities. Instead of having teachers provide instruction to teach students with disabilities these student-directed learning strategies, peers can do so. For one thing, students with disabilities may be more motivated to learn and implement the self-directed learning strategy if it is taught to them by a peer and also modeled by that peer. Gilberts et al. (2001) had peers of middle school students with disabilities teach students a self-monitoring strategy during general education class periods. Students with disabilities were able to acquire and use the self-monitoring strategy within the classroom. Gilberts et al. (pp. 34–35) suggested several recommendations with regard to peers teaching students with disabilities to self-monitor:

1. Train peer mentors. The risk associated with peers as tutors or teachers is that the relationship between the peer tutor and the student with the disability becomes unequal and actually impedes the potential for social inclusion. Peers need to be trained not only on how to teach the strategy, but how to do so in a manner that creates a peer-to-peer relationship.

2. Monitor the peer-mediated learning situations until it is evident that peer tutors have acquired the capacity to both teach the strategy and do so in a socially valuable manner. Once this is evident, do intermittent checks to make sure the situation is still positive.

3. Provide options for peer tutors to come together to talk about strategies and discuss how they have solved problems.

4. Create noninstructional opportunities for peers and students with disabilities to interact.

The Kentucky Peer Service Learning Project is one in which nondisabled peers work with same-age peers with disabilities to implement the Self-Determined Learning Model of Instruction. Although there has not been a lot of research on peers teaching students to use the whole array of student-directed learning strategies, as well as to teach goal setting or problem solving, this seems a promising avenue. For more information on this project, see http://www.ihdi.uky.edu/kypslp/index.asp.

7

Assessing Student Needs and Evaluating Programs

Assessment and instruction go hand in hand in the education of all students. In this chapter, we overview assessment procedures that can be used to determine student needs for instruction, and we return to the topic of empowerment evaluation as a program evaluation tool introduced in Chapter 3.

ASSESSING INSTRUCTIONAL NEEDS IN SELF-DETERMINATION

It is important to note that the assessment of instructional needs in self-determination needs to embody key features that may not be components of traditional academic assessment activities. That is, assessment in self-determination should be based within an empowerment evaluation framework (discussed later in this chapter), be future oriented, employ multiple measurement techniques that include participant self-report indicators, and involve key stakeholders in the process.

Determining instructional and curricular needs in the area of self-determination will involve a combination of standardized and informal procedures incorporating input from multiple sources, including the student, his or her family, professionals, and others. Informal procedures will be similar to those described by Clark (1996) with regard to transition assessment.

Clark identified informal assessment, from which transition-related decisions can be made, as including (a) situational or observational learning styles assessments; (b) curriculum-based assessment; (c) observational reports from teachers, employers, and family members; (d) situational assessments in home, community, and work settings; (e) environmental assessments; (f) personal-future planning activities; (g) structured interviews with students; (h) structured interviews with parents, guardians, advocates, or peers; (i) adaptive, behavioral, or functional skill inventories; (j) social histories; (k) employability, independent living, and personal-social skills rating scales; and (1) technology or vocational education skills assessments.

These types of assessment procedures enable planners to form a complete picture of student needs, interests, and abilities by gathering input from multiple sources, and they are important for determining the same things as they pertain to the need for instruction to promote self-determination.

The Arc's Self-Determination Scale

There are a few standardized measures of self-determination and its component elements that could be used to identify instructional and curricular needs. One such standardized measure is The Arc's Self-Determination Scale (Wehmeyer & Kelchner, 1995). (The scale and information about how to obtain the Procedural Guidelines, which describe administration and scoring procedures, are provided in Resource B and are also available online at the University of Kansas Beach Center on Disability Web site at http://www.beachcenter.org. Full instructions for accessing the scale online are available in Resource B.) This scale is a 72-item self-report measure that provides data on each of the four essential characteristics of self-determination identified by Wehmeyer and colleagues as defining self-determined behaviors, as described in Chapter 1. The scale measures (1) student autonomy, including the student's independence and the degree to which he or she acts on the basis of personal beliefs, values, interests, and abilities; (2) student self-regulation, including interpersonal cognitive problem solving, goal setting, and task performance; (3) psychological empowerment; and (4) student self-realization.

The Arc's Self-Determination Scale was normed with 500 students with and without cognitive disabilities in rural, urban, and suburban school districts across five U.S. states. The scale has been used to conduct research into the relationship between self-determination and positive adult outcomes (Wehmeyer & Schwartz, 1997) and quality-of-life variables (Wehmeyer & Schwartz, 1998), the relationship between self-determination and environmental factors (Wehmeyer & Bolding, 1999, 2001), and to validate instructional strategies to promote self-determination (Wehmeyer et al., 2000) and materials to promote student-directed transition planning (Wehmeyer & Lawrence, 1995). However, the primary purpose of the scale is to enable students with disabilities to self-assess strengths and limitations in the area of self-determination and to provide students and teachers a tool with which they can jointly determine goals and instructional programming to promote self-determination, as described next.

Use of The Arc's Self-Determination Scale

The Arc's Self-Determination Scale was designed to be a tool to enable and empower students to become more self-determined by providing a vehicle by which they can, with appropriate supports and accommodations, (a) evaluate their beliefs about themselves and their self-determination, (b) work collaboratively with educators and others to identify individual areas of strength and limitations related to self-determination goals and objectives, and (c) self-assess progress in self-determination over time.

The voices of students with disabilities are often the least frequently heard or solicited in the educational planning, decision-making, and program implementation process, as discussed in Chapter 6. The Arc's Self-Determination Scale was conceptualized as a vehicle to reverse this trend by providing a self-report indicator of self-determination. The intent of the process is first and foremost to provide a voice for students with disabilities in this important area.

One potential use of The Arc's Self-Determination Scale is to generate discussion about items the student finds interesting, problematic, or wants to discuss more broadly. Ideally, a student could use the scale with minimal instruction from a teacher or another person. However, students will vary considerably in the level of support they need to complete the assessment. Many students with mild levels of cognitive disabilities should be able to work through the scale independently or semi-independently. This process, in and of itself, has merit. Our experiences with the scale indicated that students were motivated to engage in the activity because it focused on their interests, abilities, and feelings. On numerous occasions, students indicated that no one had ever asked them about their feelings about control over and choices in their lives. If students are particularly sensitive about or focused on "scores" and "comparisons" between themselves and others, the scale could be completed, not scored, and each topic area could form the basis for discussion about students' beliefs, desires, abilities, limitations, and future plans.

A second use of the scale involves scoring it and comparing total, domain, and subdomain scores with Scale norms and, more important, examining individual strengths and weaknesses across the domains. The normed data are provided only as a point of comparison, not so that students who perform below the mean should feel a sense of failure or otherwise use the information in a pejorative manner. Normed data can provide students and teachers with honest feedback on which to base future interventions. One reason that students lack self-determination is that they experience overprotection from family members and school personnel. If students invest in the assessment process as something they want to do to benefit themselves, they will use information comparing their performance with that of others as a call to action. It is critical that the teacher or person working with the student provide feedback that directs the student toward this conclusion. Otherwise, they may use the information to reinforce feelings of insecurity and failure. The educational literature shows quite clearly that students learn from "failure" experiences when such experiences are mitigated and students are enabled to repeat the experience with success. Less than optimal performances in any area of The Arc's Self-Determination Scale should be followed by learning opportunities and experiences that enable the student to make progress in that particular area.

In this light, students could work collaboratively with the teacher to score the assessment (because of the need to make the assessment usable as a research tool, its scoring is most likely too complex for self-scoring) and discuss the outcomes, both in comparison with data from Scale norms and looking at individual student strengths and areas of need. During this process, teachers should refer back to the questions used in each domain and subdomain to find examples for students to understand what they do well and where they might need work. Such discussions should be supportive, positive, and empowering, not negative and disempowering. While seemingly paradoxical, poor performances on The Arc's Self-Determination Scale could be empowering. Individuals who are placed in control or charge of solving their own problems feel empowered. It is not students' performance, per se, that is important, but the opportunity to set them in control of their learning experience.

Any use of The Arc's Self-Determination Scale with individual students should focus on potential educational goals and objectives. This discussion, in turn, can consider possible educational programs and activities to address and meet these goals and objectives.

Self-Determination Assessment Battery

A second assessment option is the Self-Determination Assessment Battery developed by Field, Hoffman, and Sawilowsky (2004). The Self-Determination Assessment Battery contains multiple tools that measure cognitive, affective, and behavioral factors related to self-determination. In addition, these factors are assessed from the perspectives of the student, the teacher, and the parent. This battery of instruments was developed to assess knowledge, behavior, and affective components of self-determination from these varied perspectives and within the context of the Field and Hoffman (1994) model discussed in Chapter 1.

There are five instruments in the Self-Determination Assessment Battery (Field et al., 2004). Each instrument is described below.

1. Self-Determination Knowledge Scale Pretest, forms A & B

2. Self-Determination Parent Perception Scale

3. Self-Determination Teacher Perception Scale

4. Self-Determination Observation Checklist

5. Self-Determination Student Scale

Self-Determination Knowledge Scale (SDKS) Pretest

The SDKS pretest and SDKS posttest are 37-item structured response instruments designed to assess the student's cognitive knowledge of self-determination skills as taught in the Hoffman and Field (2006) *Steps to Self-Determination* curriculum. Approximately one third of the items are in true-false format, and the remaining items are multiple-choice questions. The reading level for these instruments is approximately fifth grade, enabling their use with students with mild to moderate cognitive disabilities.

Self-Determination Parent Perception Scale (PPS) and Teacher Perception Scale (TPS)

The PPS and TPS are 30-item questionnaires that are administered to parents and teachers, respectively. The items in these questionnaires were also derived from the Field and Hoffman (1994) model of self-determination. The teacher or parent rates their student or child on a 5-point Lickert scale of 0 = low to 4 = high on a variety of behaviors, abilities, and skills associated with self-determination.

Self-Determination Observation Checklist (SDOC)

The SDOC, which was discussed in Chapter 5, is a 38-item behavioral observation checklist designed to be administered by classroom teachers or other appropriate personnel in the school environment. The student is observed for approximately five minutes during a class period. Behaviors that correlate to self-determination are checked.

Self-Determination Student Scale (SDSS)

The SDSS is a 92-item self-report instrument that measures both affective and cognitive aspects of the student's self-determination. The items contain a brief stimulus, to which the student marks "That's me" or "That's not me." The SDSS yields a variety of subscale scores, including General Positive, General Negative, Specific Positive, and Specific Negative. The general subscales relate to a student's sense of global self-determination, while the specific subscales relate primarily to application in their education, home, and related environmental settings. The positive subscales indicate self-determination in areas of perceived strength, while the negative subscales indicate areas of perceived weakness in self-determination.

The Self-Determination Assessment Battery instruments have many possible uses in education. First, they can be used to assist in educational planning. Because the instruments take into account the perspectives of the student, teacher, and parent, it is possible to identify areas of similarity and discrepancy among these three perspectives. This may provide insight to students regarding their functioning in different areas of their lives or how they are perceived in different situations. For example, a parent's ratings of his or her child may differ from those given by the teacher. This provides an opportunity for discussion among the student, teacher, and parent to determine the reasons for this discrepancy. It may be that the student is exhibiting skills in the home that he or she is not displaying at school, or it may be that the teacher and the parent were using different criteria to evaluate the student's performance. The discussion that can be generated from examining these differences can provide important feedback for the student and can lead to determining appropriate instructional interventions.

Just as students are being rated from three different perspectives (i.e., student, teacher, and parent), they are also being assessed in three different areas: cognition/knowledge, behavior, and affect. Examining the differences in the three different areas helps to determine appropriate interventions. For example, a student's results may indicate knowledge of important self-determination concepts and a low level of behaviors associated with self-determination. This may indicate the need for experiences in the school and community where the student has the opportunity to apply the skills with coaching and support provided by the school.

The instruments clearly have varied uses for educational planning, both as a discussion tool in educational planning meetings that can help to promote greater self-awareness and as a tool that can help to identify appropriate educational interventions. In addition, the instruments can be used for program evaluation or research purposes. By using the instruments as pre- and posttests before and after an instructional intervention, data can be obtained that can help to assess the effectiveness of the intervention. (Information on ordering the Self-Determination Assessment Battery can be obtained from the Wayne State University Center for Self-Determination and Transition Business Office at 313/ 577–1638 or sdtalk@wayne.edu.)

The AIR Self-Determination Scale

Another measure of self-determination is the AIR Self-Determination Scale (Wolman, Campeau, Dubois, Mithaug, & Stolarski, 1994), which is based on theoretical work by Mithaug and colleagues (see Wehmeyer et al., 2003) and measures individual capacity for, and opportunity to practice, self-determination. There are educator, student, and parent forms of the scale, and the results of each can be used to develop a profile of a student's level of self-determination, identify areas of strength and areas needing improvement, identify educational goals and objectives, and develop strategies to build student capacity and increase students' opportunities to become self-determined. (The AIR Self-Determination Scales are available for free online at the University of Oklahoma Zarrow Center for Learning Web site at http://www.ou.edu/zarrow/sdetermination.html)

PROGRAM EVALUATION

While the establishment of goals and criteria to measure student progress on such goals has always been a primary function of the Individualized Education Program (IEP) process, this has not often been approached at the level of program evaluation as opposed to student evaluation. That is, goals were written and criteria set to judge student performance, and any failure to achieve these goals was interpreted as a problem with or for the student. Goals were set to judge students, not programs. As emphasized in Chapters 3 and 5, however, program evaluation should be an integral part of educational planning and decision making.

Program evaluation refers, quite simply, to efforts to evaluate the efficacy and utility of a given program, in this case, the student's educational program. One conducts program evaluations to gather information about the program's plans, activities, and outcomes that can contribute to the modification and improvement of the program. In the case of a student's educational program, the stakeholders who are internal to the program include the student, his or her family, school personnel, community members, and, generally, members of the IEP team. One program evaluation model, called Empowerment Evaluation, lends itself to promoting self-determination.

Empowerment Evaluation

Empowerment evaluation was defined by its developers as

the use of evaluation concepts, techniques, and findings to foster improvement and self-determination. It employs both qualitative and quantitative methodologies. Although is can be applied to individuals, organizations, communities, and societies or cultures, the focus is on programs. It is attentive to empowering processes and outcomes. (Fetterman, 1996, p. 4)

The empowerment evaluation framework has been used widely across program and policy spectrums, including being used to evaluate programs in substance abuse prevention, welfare reform, HIV prevention, school reform, and crime prevention (Fetterman, 1996). Moreover, the empowerment evaluation approach is well grounded in evaluation theory and practice, having been "institutionalized within the American Evaluation Association" (p. 3) and embodying the spirit of standards developed by the Joint Committee on Standards for Educational Evaluation.

Unlike traditional program evaluation, the empowerment evaluation process has

an unambiguous value orientation—it is designed to help people help themselves and improve their programs using a form of self-evaluation and reflection. Program participants conduct their own evaluations and typically act as facilitators; an outside evaluator often serves as a coach or additional facilitator depending on the internal program capabilities. (Fetterman, 1996, p. 5)

Fetterman (1996) continued, stating that empowerment evaluation is, by necessity, "a collaborative group activity, not an individual pursuit" and noting that "an evaluator does not and cannot empower anyone; people empower themselves, often with assistance and coaching" (p. 5). Fetterman further contended that because of the democratic nature of the empowerment evaluation process, the intent or purpose of the process changes. Traditional program evaluation emphasizes and results in an evaluation of the program's value and utility. That judgment is the endpoint of the program evaluation process. In empowerment evaluation, however, the determination of a program's utility becomes an indicator on which to improve the program. Fetterman stated, "Program participants learn to continually assess their progress toward self-determined goals and to reshape their plans and strategies according to this assessment. In the process, self-determination is fostered, illumination generated, and liberation actualized" (p. 6).

Implementing an Empowerment Evaluation Process

Fetterman and colleagues identified several steps of the empowerment evaluation process. The following steps could provide a framework for IEP teams to make evaluation decisions and improve a student's educational program.

Step 1: Taking stock. The first step in the empowerment evaluation process involves having program participants, in this case, all members of the IEP team, including the student, rate the program (e.g., the student's educational program) on a scale of 1 to 10, with 10 indicating the highest level of quality and satisfaction. Because it is often more useful to compartmentalize programs, team members may identify several specific activities or portions of the educational program and rate them separately. Program participants are also asked to document their ratings. The importance of this step is tied not specifically to the rating assigned but to the establishment of baseline information and the opportunity this process provides to allow each participant to express his or her perception of the quality of the program. Fetterman also noted that this process often illustrates or reinforces the necessity of collecting data to either support or refute some of the perceptions.

Step 2: Setting goals. The second step of the process is to have program participants indicate how highly they would like to rate their program in the future and set goals that will lead them to that rating. This goal-setting activity is at the level of improving the program, not specifically related to setting educational goals for the student's IEP. That is, the goal setting is intended to identify ways, overall, that the program might improve. Returning to the potential use of this process in an IEP team setting, the team might decide that one component of improving the quality of the student's overall educational program might involve securing some specialized training for the student's teacher, and set a goal to make that happen. It might be that a particular assistive device or physical accommodation is necessary to improve the educational program, and as such, the team would put in place goals and an action plan to achieve that. The IEP team might determine that the general curriculum is too narrowly defined for their particular district, and they might set a goal to address issues of universal design in that curriculum. These are IEP team goals, not student goals.

Step 3: Developing strategies. As a third step, program participants are responsible for developing strategies to achieve overall program objectives. At the level of the educational planning process, this is the determination of the appropriate curriculum and the design of relevant educational supports, including the determination of instructional goals for students.

Step 4: Documenting progress. In this step, program participants are asked what types of documentation are needed to provide evidence of progress at two levels: progress on the IEP or system goals identified in Step 2, and progress on the specific content or programmatic goals and strategies identified in Step 3.

The reason to engage in program evaluation is, quite simply, to ensure that programmatic efforts to promote self-determination are effective.

Family Support for Self-Determination

I t will come as no surprise to you when we point out that family members play a key role in supporting students in their development of knowledge and skills for self-determination and in their efforts to express their self-determination. Throughout this book, we have emphasized the importance of positive, nurturing relationships to self-determination. When it comes to promoting or discouraging a sense of self-determination, there are typically no relationships more important than those that students have with their parents and other family members.

The relationship between parent and child will affect the student's self-determination, and in turn, the student's efforts to be self-determined will often have an impact on other family members. Psychologists often view families as systems, where the actions of each individual affect what happens to others in the system. A family system can be compared to a mobile. If we envision a mobile and think about each family member as a part of the mobile, we find that moving one part of the mobile results in every other part of the mobile moving as well. As students endeavor to become more self-determined, they will have an impact on their parents and other family members. As parents make shifts in either their efforts to be self-determined or in the ways they interact with their children, this will also create shifts for their sons and daughters (Turnbull & Turnbull, 1996).

In this chapter, we examine ways in which family members affect student self-determination. We will identify specific ways parents can support their sons and daughters in becoming more self-determined. Finally, we will provide some tips and suggestions for parents for incorporating self-determination concepts into their parenting.

HOW FAMILIES IMPACT STUDENT SELF-DETERMINATION

According to Turnbull and Turnbull (1996), there are four features of families that affect student self-determination. These four features, which either encourage or limit self-determination, are listed and briefly discussed below.

1. Family characteristics, such as characteristics of the disability, cultural values, beliefs and expectations, and coping styles. Each family is unique, and the characteristics that make each family unique will affect the ways in which that family can best support the self-determination of each family member. For example, the needs of families and the ways they can provide support for self-determination will be different for families with a member who has a severe cognitive impairment than they are for families who have a member with a hearing impairment. Similarly, the type of self-determination support a family provides will be affected by their cultural background. For example, the level of connection between parent and child and the extent to which adult children are expected to live separately from their families often vary by culture. These cultural beliefs will have an impact on the ways families support self-determination.

In seeking to find ways to help families support self-determination for their sons and daughters, it important to develop an understanding of the individual strengths and needs of each family. Turnbull and Turnbull (1996) elaborated on this concept when they made the following statement:

> A fundamental consideration in working on self-determination with families is the assumption that because all families vary, the approach with each family must be as individualized, like the approach with each student. Having a prototypical "ideal family" in mind and judging all families against that prototype is a strategy that brings only frustration and failure. A key for success is not only recognizing family diversity, but indeed honoring it and taking it fully into account when designing self-determination training, supports and services. (p. 216)

Turnbull and Turnbull (2001, p. 66) outlined the following guidelines to build a bridge between the value systems and practices of families and educators. Their model is based on the posture of cultural reciprocity developed by Kalyanpur and Harry (1999).

A. Learn about the family's strengths, needs, and expectations that evolve from the "family story." Also find out the priorities and preferences for their child's educational program—Individualized Education Program (IEP), placement-related services, extra-curricular activities, and so on. Seek to understand and honor the cultural values and priorities as you establish a reliable alliance with them.

B. Converse with the family about the assumptions that underlie the cultural values and priorities. Seek to find out about their rationales.

C. As you reflect on their priorities and preferences, identify any disagreements or alternative perspectives that you or other professionals have, as compared to those of the family, associated with providing educational supports and services to the student, the family, or both.

D. Find out whether the family being served recognizes and values these assumptions and, if not, how their views differ from those of the professional.

E. Acknowledge and give explicit respect to any cultural differences identified, and fully explain the cultural basis of the professional assumptions.

F. Through discussion and collaboration, set about determining the most effective way of adapting professional interpretations or recommendations to the value system of this family.

The experience of one special education teacher in applying these steps is provided in the following case study to illustrate (a) how these steps can be used to increase understanding of a family's unique characteristics and (b) how to use that understanding to promote a greater sense of self-determination for students and their families.

Applying Cultural Reciprocity
Guidelines to Promote Self-Determination
for Students and Their Families: A Case Example

Amanda Ward is a white, non-Hispanic, special education teacher in a suburban community in the Midwest. She graduated from college two years ago and is working with 18- to 26-year-olds in a transition program. This is her first job. She enjoys her work and is planning to begin a graduate program in special education very shortly. This is her experience with Cindy, one of her older students. Cindy is 22 years old. Amanda told us the following story about her experience with Cindy.

Cindy works 40 hours a week and gets paid very well. She also gets benefits. She lives with her father who, as he states it, is from the "old country" with what he calls his "good old values." Cindy wants to move out of her father's house. He wants to keep her at home. He likes having her around and says that she is too young to be alone without a husband to take care of her, and anyway, she would get lonely. Every time we meet to talk, her father seems set in what he wants and is doing. His idea for a compromise is to build a house behind his own for Cindy. She can move away, but then still be on the property. In my second job, I work with adults with developmental disabilities who live in their own apartments. I suggested to the father that we go over there and see what they can do living alone. He will not go with me, saying that those are not his values, they are new-fangled modern values, and they will not work with his family.

Following the model of cultural reciprocity, Amanda took the following steps:

1. She identified her own values about the situation. Amanda's professional interpretation was that Cindy was capable and should be living on her own. Amanda needed to consider the cultural values embedded in that interpretation, what she believed about independence for young people, and what her beliefs were about autonomy and dependence issues for women.

2. Amanda identified the discrepancies between her values, Cindy's values, and Cindy's father's values about Cindy living on her own. She asked Cindy's father about the values affecting his worry about Cindy's vulnerability and need for someone to take care of her, and she asked Cindy questions about why she wanted to live on her own. She tried to understand that their values were based on their culture and time of origin.

3. In a meeting with Cindy and her father, Amanda identified the beliefs each of them had about the situation. She tried to make explicit and understand as fully as possible the reasoning behind each of their beliefs. As a team, the three of them identified ways in which assumptions made by any of them might not

be rooted in the reality of the situation (e.g., maybe Cindy didn't need to earn money to support herself, as her father was willing to support her; maybe some fears that Cindy's father had about Cindy living on her own in the community were not rooted in the reality of the community in which they were currently living; maybe the likely reality of what Cindy imagined about her living on her own was different from the way she visualized it).

4. Amanda acknowledged and demonstrated respect for the values of each person involved in the transition planning team. The three of them talked about where their values differed and where they were in agreement. Amanda helped Cindy and her father discuss alternative solutions that helped both of them negotiate this important transition. They discussed the following questions: What is the minimum need that each of them must have in any solution? What are some alternatives that allow for each feeling that their minimum need is met? Could they choose one or two to think about until the next meeting? They decided that Cindy finding a place to live that was close to her father, with daily phone calls and several visits each week, would be a goal for Cindy that they could all support.

2. Family interactions, such as role expectations, relationships, cohesion, and adaptability. Not only do families function as a system, but there are also several subsystems within the system of the family. The way in which different members of the family relate to each other (e.g., husband and wife; sisters and brothers; grandparents and parents; grandparents and children) will affect the way in which the family functions as a whole. Families vary in the boundaries they set with each other and the ways in which they adapt to each other. According to Turnbull and Turnbull (1996),

A key concept of family interactions is that there are multiple and competing priorities, responsibilities, and resources within the family system. The self-determination of the individual with a disability can best be supported by taking into account the needs and strengths of other individuals and subsystems. . . . When working with individuals and families, it is extremely helpful to have a sense of the family's place along the continuum of cohesion and adaptability. By reflecting consideration for the closeness and distance of family boundaries (cohesion) and the abilities of families to make changes (adaptability), self-determination supports and services can be far more responsive. (p. 216)

3. **Family functions, including economic, daily care, recreation, socialization, affective, educational or vocational, and self-definition needs.** Families have many responsibilities. The burdens, pressures, and time demands on today's families are frequent topics in popular magazines and self-help books. As we write this book, we are keenly aware of the multiple responsibilities we have within our families and know what it is like to try to meet those responsibilities and keep them in balance.

When working with families to develop support for students' self-determination, it is essential that we remain mindful of the numerous responsibilities families face. Families will have more energy and resources to devote to encouraging self-determination for their sons and daughters if we do not overload them with expectations. Promoting family-friendly, school-home collaboration can help conserve family resources. For example, providing multiple options for conference times that allow family members flexibility in scheduling is one example of providing support in a family-friendly manner. Other examples of family-friendly practices include providing child care for siblings when parent support sessions are offered, asking for input from parent advisory councils on parent support issues to ensure consideration of logistical issues parents face, and helping parents learn how to incorporate support for self-determination into existing daily routines. Instructional support for self-determined parenting (discussed later in this chapter) is aimed at helping parents juggle multiple demands while increasing their ability to promote self-determination in their sons and daughters (and themselves).

4. **Family life span issues, including developmental stages of family interactions and functions over time and transitions or changes in family characteristics, composition, cohesion, and function.** Families encounter the most stress during periods of change (Turnbull & Turnbull, 1996). The emphasis on self-determination originated in the transition from school to community movement. As a result, most of the interventions and strategies developed for self-determination were intended for use as students are preparing to graduate from school, leave, and move on to adult responsibilities. Clearly, the transition years are a time of great change for the family and, as a result, typically a time of high stress. Turnbull and Turnbull suggested that expectations of family support for self-determination might best be established around "periods of calm" when there is not as much change occurring in the family. This suggestion provides a good reason for including self-determination instruction and support in early childhood, elementary, and middle school settings, as well as during the more common time of high school. This does not mean that support for self-determination should not be provided

during the transition period. To the contrary, it is essential to focus on self-determination as students are beginning to exercise more adult responsibility. However, if a foundation for self-determination is laid during the early years, supports for further development and expression of self-determination during the high school and early adult years are much more likely to be successful.

STRATEGIES AND RESOURCES TO HELP FAMILY MEMBERS LEARN ABOUT SELF-DETERMINATION

Just as we shouldn't expect students and teachers to learn about self-determination without direct instruction related to the knowledge, skills, and beliefs for self-determination, we shouldn't expect parents and other family members to understand the concept of self-determination and how best to support it. An important tenet of adult learning theory is that adult learning will be most successful if learners are encouraged to fit new learning into their current understanding and life experience. Because self-determination is a concept with which we all have some experience, instructional and support opportunities for parents should build on what they already know about self-determination from their own life experience. It should also encourage parents to build on their knowledge of their son or daughter, which has likely been gained over a longer period of time and with a higher degree of passion than it has been for any other member of the team.

There are a variety of ways in which parents can learn about self-determination and how to support self-determination for their sons and daughters. Several self-determination instructional programs encourage parent participation in the program with their sons and daughters. For example, *Steps to Self-Determination* (Hoffman & Field, 2006) provides guidelines for including parent involvement in a self-determination workshop that introduces the concept of self-determination to adolescents and their parents. The workshop provides activities for parents and their sons or daughters to complete together in areas such as self-awareness and acceptance. *Steps to Self-Determination* also includes several optional activities for students and their parents to complete as homework. By involving parents in instructional activities, the family members learn more about self-determination and how they can best support self-determination while, at the same time, helping their sons and daughters develop their knowledge and awareness for self-determination.

The *Self-Determined Learning Model for Early Elementary Students: A Parent's Guide* (Palmer & Wehmeyer, 2002) provides introductory information for parents about self-determination. It also provides specific instructional activities parents can use with their children to help them learn how to use the Self-Determined Learning Model of Instruction. Specific sections of the book are devoted to problem-solving, communication, and self-advocacy skills and self-management. Examples of how parents can implement instructional activities within each of these areas are provided. In addition, a list of children's books related to each element of the self-determined learning model is included.

The TAKE CHARGE for the Future curriculum (Powers et al., 2004; see also Table 3.3) includes monthly community-based workshops for youth, parents, and mentors as well as telephone and home visit support for parents. This curriculum includes a video, also titled TAKE CHARGE. The video includes interviews with four youth and their parents, providing a personal look at parents' reactions to their sons and daughters becoming more self-determined as well as providing insight on ways parents can encourage self-determination. The video has been used by some teachers to begin a discussion with parents about self-determination. Discussions have revolved around what self-determination is and why it's important. These sessions have also provided opportunities for parents to talk about the impact that student self-determination has on their relationships with their children and how family members can foster self-determination.

An instructional program that helps parents learn about the concept of self-determination and apply those concepts to their parenting is *Self-Determined Parenting* (Field, Hoffman, & Les, 2006). This program includes three instructional modules, each lasting two hours. The modules can be combined into a day's workshop or offered in separate sessions. The program helps parents understand key components of self-determination and presents evidence-based strategies for effective parenting. Within the framework of self-determination, it provides a process to help parents make decisions about the types of parenting strategies that are the best fit for their families. The primary focus of *Self-Determined Parenting* is on helping parents to apply self-determination skills in their lives so they can be more effective parents and role models of self-determination for their children. The program also provides some suggestions for ways parents can support development of knowledge and skills for self-determination in their daughters and sons.

In addition to the curricular materials available to help parents and other family members learn about self-determination, there are several resources available on Web sites and through other electronic media to help family members learn about self-determination and how they can best support self-determination in their sons and daughters. These resources are briefly described below.

- The Web site for the PACER Center (http://www.pacer.org), a resource center for parents of children, youth, and adults with disabilities, has several practical information resources on self-determination targeted to parents. The site includes basic information that will help parents become more familiar with the concept of self-determination. It also provides links to specific resources that parents can use to promote self-determination. It has several excellent resources for parents on encouraging self-determination through the IEP process.

- The Web site for the Beach Center on Disability at the University of Kansas (http://www.beachcenter.org) provides 20 articles on self-determination. Parents can easily scroll through the titles of these articles to find the types of information they would like to obtain. Articles on topics such as family support for self-directed IEPs, research on self-determination, and cultural issues impacting self-determination are provided. Visitors to this site will also find real-life stories about efforts of individuals and their families to promote self-determination. Several tip sheets for families on how they can support self-determination for their sons and daughters are available at this site.

- The Web site of the National Dissemination Center for Children With Disabilities (http://www.nichcy.org) provides many self-determination resources and tools for parents. A couple of their most popular products are *A Student's Guide to the IEP* and a *Technical Assistance Guide to the IEP*, as discussed in Chapter 3 and featured in Table 3.3. This set of materials was designed to help students develop their own IEPs and to assist individuals (including parents and teachers) who would like to help students play a more central role in their IEP. This program includes an audiotape that features several students talking about their experiences as active participants in their IEP teams. On the flip side of the tape is a program for adults who wish to support students' efforts to be more actively involved in their IEPs (e.g., parents, teachers, adult agency representatives). All of these materials can be downloaded from the Web site. Other resources related to self-determination on the NICHCY Web site include links to other Web sites that provide information on self-determination, listings of conferences where information on self-determination will be provided, and several additional publications on self-determination and transition-related topics.

- As an advocacy group for persons with intellectual and developmental disabilities, The Arc has posted several position and policy statements on self-determination at its Web site (http://www.TheArc.org). Family members who wish to learn more about ways in which a focus on self-determination can be infused into programs and services for disabilities can find valuable information at this site.

- *Self-Determination Technical Assistance Resources Start-up (STARS)* (Field, 2006): The purpose of this CD is to provide informational resources on self-determination for family members, adult agency representatives, and educators. The CD includes a variety of resources, including an introductory PowerPoint presentation about the basics of self-determination that can be used either as a self-study tool or as a presentation tool to help others learn about self-determination. The CD includes a section specifically for parents. In this section, parents will find basic information on self-determination, tips and strategies for ways they can encourage self-determination in their sons and daughters, and real-life examples describing families' efforts to promote self-determination for their sons and daughters with disabilities.

FAMILY SUPPORT FOR SELF-DETERMINATION: TIPS AND TOOLS

As family members learn about self-determination, it is important that they put what they are learning into action if their new information is going to have an impact on the ability of their sons and daughters to be self-determined. In this section, we provide some practical strategies parents can use to encourage self-determination. Parents should consider these suggestions in the context of the needs of their sons and daughters, their specific family dynamics, and their parenting styles to make determinations about what might or might not work for them. We encourage parents to try out different strategies and use the self-determination process to reflect on and learn what works well and what doesn't work for them and their sons or daughters.

Davis and Wehmeyer (1991) provided these specific "10 steps to self-determination" for parents of children with disabilities:

1. Walk the tightrope between protection and independence. Allow your son or daughter to explore his or her world. This may mean biting your lip and watching from the kitchen window when your child first meets the neighbor's kids, instead of running out to supervise. While there are obvious limits to this, all parents have to "let go," and it is never easy.

2. Children need to learn that what they say or do is important and can have an influence on others. This involves allowing risk taking and exploration. Encourage your child to ask questions and express opinions. Involvement in family discussions and decision-making sessions is one way of providing this opportunity to learn.

3. Self-worth and self-confidence are critical factors in the development of self-determination. Model your own sense of positive self-esteem to your child. Tell your child that she is important by spending time with her. Again, involve her in family activities and in family decisions.

4. Don't run away from questions from your child about differences related to his disability. That doesn't mean, however, to focus on the negative side of the condition. Stress that everyone is individual, encourage your child's unique abilities, and help him to accept unavoidable limitations.

5. Recognize the process of reaching goals; don't just emphasize outcomes. Children need to learn to work toward goals. For older children, encourage skills like organization and goal setting by modeling these behaviors. Make lists or hang a marker board in the laundry room showing the daily schedule for each family member. Talk about the steps you are going to use to complete a task, and involve them in tasks leading to family goals, such as planning for a vacation.

6. Schedule opportunities for interactions with children of different ages and backgrounds. This could be in day care centers, schools, churches, and when playing in the neighborhood. Start early in finding opportunities for your son or daughter to participate in activities that help all children realize that everyone is unique.

7. Set realistic but ambitious expectations. The adage that our goals should extend just beyond our reach is true here. Take an active role in your child's educational experience. Be familiar with his or her reading ability and identify books that provide enough challenge to move to the next reading level. Be sure you don't just force activities that lead to frustration, but don't assume that all of the progress should occur at school.

8. Allow your child to take responsibility for her own actions—successes and failures. Provide valid reasons for doing things, instead of simply saying, "because I said so!" Providing explanations gives the child the opportunity to make an activity his own.

9. Don't leave choice-making opportunities to chance. Take every opportunity to allow your child to make choices; what he or she wears, what is served for dinner, or where the family goes for vacation. And, although this is not always practical or possible, make sure that these choice opportunities are meaningful. For

example, for most children, choosing between broccoli and cauliflower is not a choice! Also, when offering choices, make sure that the child's decision is honored.

10. Provide honest, positive feedback. Focus on the behavior or task that needs to be changed. Don't make your child feel like a failure. For example, if your son or daughter attempts to complete a school activity, say, a math sheet, but is unable to do so, phrase the feedback so that he or she knows that the failure was specific to the worksheet and not in him or her. We all learn from our mistakes, but only if they are structured so that they do not lead us to believe that the problem is within us.

Some additional strategies parents may wish to try with their children to encourage self-determination include reading stories related to self-determination with their children, making the most of teachable moments, and acting as role models of self-determination. Each of these strategies is further discussed below.

Sharing Stories About Self-Determination

Stories can provide a powerful teaching tool. Given the importance of self-determination in our culture, there are many stories that address elements of self-determination. When we learn through stories, we have the opportunity to think about new concepts in a manner that is highly engaging, but also safe. Sharing stories between parent and child can also help promote positive, nurturing relationships, which are a key foundational element for self-determination. Stories in the form of family stories passed down by word of mouth, stories told in movies or TV shows, or stories provided in books can be highly effective in helping us learn more about what it takes to be self-determined. The level of engagement students experience with the stories can be heightened by our ability to make the stories come alive.

Learning about self-determination through stories is an activity that can easily fit into the normal rhythm of family activities. A list of books that address self-determination concepts is provided in Table 8.1. The list includes descriptions of ways in which the books address self-determination concepts. Most of the books identified in this list are children's books. However, several secondary-level teachers used the stories with adolescents and found them to be highly effective with older students as well.

Making the Most of Teachable Moments

Family members are often in particularly good situations to capitalize on teachable moments. If you are observant, you will find many opportunities

Table 8.1   Children's Books for Self-Determination

**Helping Students Learn About
Self-Determination Through Children's Literature**

Children's literature provides an excellent vehicle to illustrate self-determination concepts. Below is a listing of some children's books that can be used to supplement self-determination instruction. This list was generated by teachers who participated in the Ingham Intermediate School District (Mason, MI) Self-Determination Learning Community. Informal teachers' notes are provided throughout the listings.

Where Do Balloons Go? An Uplifting Mystery by Jamie Lee Curtis

This book ponders all of the places balloons might go when they float up to the sky. It is beautifully illustrated. It is good for supporting expansive thinking, or thinking outside the box. This book especially supports dream and creativity aspects of self-determination.

I Am—I Am a Dancer by Eleanor Schick

The book jacket states, "Celebrated here are the limitless possibilities of childhood and children's imaginations, especially the wonderful sense of being part of it all. The illustrations are simple, yet warm and engaging." This book supports dream and creativity components of self-determination.

I'm Gonna Like Me; Letting Off a Little Self-Esteem by Jamie Lee Curtis and Laura Connell

This book focuses on liking ourselves in many different types of situations. It has great illustrations that are both colorful and playful. It focuses on accepting and valuing yourself, an important concept in self-determination.

Alice and Greta by Steven J. Simmons

Alice is a good witch. Greta is a not-so-good witch. Through humor and a lighthearted approach, this book promotes the "brewmerang principle," which is defined as "Whatever you chant, whatever you brew, sooner or later comes back to you." This book supports discussion of anticipating potential results of actions, an important competency for self-determination.

Bunny Cakes by Rosemary Wells

In this story, a bunny wants to make an earthworm cake decorated with "red-hot marshmallow squirters." He is thwarted at every step he takes. However, he finally reaches his goal. This book provides an opportunity to discuss elements of self-determination including persistence and using creativity to overcome barriers.

A Bad Case of Stripes by David Shannon

This book tells the story of a girl who is always trying to fit in and be like everyone else. She has some unwelcome results and learns that she likes being herself. This book provides an excellent jumping-off point to discuss issues of self-awareness and accepting and believing in yourself.

Stephanie's Ponytail by Robert Munsch

Stephanie wears a ponytail to school for the first time and she is greeted with chants of "ugly, ugly, very ugly." Stephanie replies, "It's my ponytail and I like it that way!" The next day everyone comes to school with a ponytail. Stephanie is upset because now

---

(Continued)

Table 8.1 (Continued)

everyone is copying her. A great story is told, as Stephanie tries to find a variety of ways to be original. Self-determination components addressed include accept and value yourself, creativity, and experience outcomes and learn.

A Coat of Many Colors by Dolly Parton

This book is based on the Dolly Parton song of the same name. It tells the story of how Dolly's mother made a coat for her when she was young. Her mother sewed the coat from scraps of material, because she did not have money to buy a coat. Dolly thought the coat was beautiful, but her peers at school laughed at the coat. She tells a wonderful story about defining yourself, rather than letting others define you. Self-determination components addressed include accept and value yourself and develop and nurture positive relationships.

The City of Ember by Jeanne DuPrau

Lina and Doon live in the City of Ember, which exists in eternal darkness. The city is in danger of losing even all of their artificial light. The book tells the story of Lina and Doon as they rise to the challenge of saving the city. This is a real page-turner. Self-determination components addressed include know your strengths, weaknesses, needs, and preferences; develop and nurture positive relationships; take risks and anticipate potential consequences; creativity; realize success; compare performance to expected performance; and compare outcome to expected outcome. Age recommendations are not provided, but it appears to be geared toward upper elementary and middle school.

Giraffes Can't Dance by Giles Andreae and Guy Parker-Rees

This is an adorable story with fabulous illustrations. Gerald the Giraffe loves to dance, but his legs are too skinny and his neck is too long, and so forth. The cricket believes in Gerald and tells him, "Everything makes music if you want it to." So Gerald starts swaying to his own sweet tune. This story provides an opportunity to discuss individual strengths and differences and believing in yourself.

Salt in His Shoes by Michael Jordan, and ***In Pursuit of a Dream*** by Deloris Jordan and Roslyn M. Jordan

Michael sets goals, works hard, and is dedicated to become a good basketball player. With a little encouragement from his family and some "salt in his shoes," he does just that! This book encourages students to believe in themselves and follow their dreams. It also highlights the importance of supportive relationships.

Hooray for You! A Celebration of "You-ness" by Marianne Richmond

This story is a celebration of "You-ness"—the grand sum of body, mind, and heart that makes every person truly unique. It focuses on honoring our own individuality.

It's Okay to Be Different by Todd Parks

Illustrations and brief text describe all kinds of differences that are "okay" such as "It's okay to be adopted" or "It's okay to need some help." It can be used as a tool to have a conversation about individual strengths and weaknesses and believing in yourself.

I Knew You Could (2nd book of *The Little Engine That Could*)**

This is a classic story about all the stops you make in your life. Our teachers described it as a MUST HAVE. It teaches concepts of persistence in belief in yourself.

Oh, the Places You'll Go by Dr. Seuss

This book is an excellent resource to help students dream about a variety of future possibilities and plans.

Al Capone Does My Shirts by Gennifer Choldenko

This is a quick chapter book about a boy who moves to Alcatraz Island with his family during the 1930s. The plot revolves around Moose and his sister Natalie, who is autistic. It's a great read. Significant attention is placed on dealing with issues of disability.

Runt by Marion Dane Bauer

This book is about a young wolf cub who is named Runt by his father. He feels isolated from the group until his finds his own gift. It provides a starting point to talk about how differences can bring diversity to "the pack" and how having faith in yourself is important.

throughout the day to reflect on and learn from real experiences related to self-determination. For example, if your son or daughter is trying to decide what to wear, there is an opportunity to talk about what they are planning to do that day and how their choice of clothing can help or hinder them in reaching their goals. If you are shopping together, there is an opportunity to discuss what your son or daughter likes or dislikes and why, leading to greater self-awareness. If your child talks with you about difficulty he or she is having with a friend, there is an opportunity to discuss what he or she wants from relationships and how that can be achieved. It also provides an opportunity for you to provide coaching in relationship skills, an important ingredient for increased self-determination. Watching for, and using, teachable moments is a way family members can promote self-determination for their sons and daughters in a manner that fits naturally with typical family activities.

Providing a Positive Role Model of Self-Determination

Throughout this book, we have stressed the importance of modeling as an effective instructional strategy. We often learn as much, if not more, from what we observe than from direct instructional efforts. Parents are important role models for their children. If parents work to promote their own self-determination and talk with students about their own efforts, they will be taking an important step toward helping their sons and daughters acquire knowledge, skills, and beliefs for self-determination.

Parents play an important role in the development and the expression of their children's' self-determination. Their role is important throughout the life span, from early childhood to adulthood. Positive, nurturing relationships are central to the ability to be self-determined, and there is no relationship more important than the relationship between parent and child. In this chapter, we focused on the importance of family support for self-determination. We identified resources for parents to learn more about self-determination and find activities they can use to encourage self-determination in their children. Finally, we provided several practical tips and strategies parents can use to promote self-determination. A key element for parents to promote greater self-determination is for them to foster their own self-determination. By focusing on their own self-determination, parents can provide appropriate role models of self-determination for their children. In addition, the tools of self-determination will help parents make decisions about the types of support strategies that work best for them and their families.

Nurturing the Self-Determination of Teachers

Self-determination has clearly become a fundamental concept in special education and disability services. A focus on self-determination is essential to providing high-quality, effective educational experiences for students, with or without disabilities.

If a focus on self-determination is important for students to achieve at their optimum levels, shouldn't it be important for teachers and administrators as well? Our answer to this question is a resounding "yes." Self-determination is important for teachers and administrators for the following reasons:

Self-determination skills are essential to designing and implementing effective instruction.

Self-determination skills are critical to effectively participate in the school improvement process.

To learn self-determination skills, students need self-determined role models.

Student self-determination is enhanced when educators share a strong philosophical foundation about the need to promote self-determination throughout the culture of the school.

Self-determined teachers and administrators make a positive difference in the climate, morale, and synergy in a school. (Field, 1998)

When writing about the importance of self-determination for teachers, many authors have emphasized the importance that teachers play as role models for students. Just as the little girl who hears the words "no, no" frequently is likely to be observed telling her dog "no, no," the actions of teachers often speak louder than their words when it comes to what students learn about self-determination. Powers (1997) wrote, "Modeling is a critical ingredient for bolstering self-determination and it is essential that teachers have the information, skills, and supports necessary to function as instructors and role models for youth" (p. 1). Martin (1997) emphasized the importance of modeling in self-determination when he stated, "Teacher self-determined behavior does indeed impact student self-determination. This comes through in every-day student-teacher interactions, plus in how teachers model their own self-determination" (p. 2).

Beyond the importance of educators' role as models for students, the ability to be self-determined helps educators be more effective in their jobs. Earlier in this book, we discussed research demonstrating that self-determination is positively linked to higher levels of motivation, goal attainment, and greater quality of life and well-being. This research should guide the types of education and supports we provide for educators (e.g., initial preparation, staff development, performance appraisal processes, mentoring programs) just as it does the student educational process. Just as students' learning and achievement are enhanced when they are active participants in the educational process and when they are able to see the importance of what they are learning relative to their personal values, learning and job success for teachers are enhanced when they are able to engage in the activities of their work in a self-determined manner. For example, teachers who are self-determined adapt and enhance the curriculum to use it in a way that best meets the needs of students in their classes and fits best with their teaching styles. *Steps to Self-Determination* (Hoffman & Field, 2006) contains numerous examples from teachers of ways in which they used their self-determination to enhance the implementation of self-determination instructional efforts. Some examples of ways in which self-determined teachers found innovative ways to implement self-determination curricula in their classrooms, despite many barriers, are found in Table 9.1.

Because an emphasis on self-determination leads to increased internal motivation (Ryan & Deci, 2000), promoting self-determination for staff should lead to increased motivation for teachers toward their work. When teachers and administrators have higher levels of motivation, they are more likely to increase their overall effectiveness with students. In addition, a self-determination focus in administrator and teacher preparation supports proactive rather than reactive teaching and management styles.

Table 9.1 Teacher Self-Determination in Curriculum Implementation

Self-Determination Component	Ms. B. Special Education Resource Room Teacher	Ms. C. Alternative Education Teacher	Mr. M. Language Arts Teacher
Know Yourself	Ms. B. knew her strengths as a teacher. One of those strengths included significant skills in designing and implementing outdoor adventure challenge activities.	It was a difficult school year for Ms. C. There was a great deal of change occurring in her district and multiple demands on her time. She wanted to implement the new self-determination curriculum, but she also knew that her time and energy for a new curriculum focus were limited.	Mr. M. reviewed the *Steps to Self-Determination* curriculum and decided that he would like to use it in conjunction with his creative writing class. He thought there was a significant amount of overlap between the concepts taught in the *Steps* curriculum and the objectives for the creative writing class. In addition, he believed the process of creative writing would fit well with self-determination.
Value Yourself	Ms. B. believed in her ability to create effective lessons using outdoor adventure challenge principles. She also recognized the value that outdoor adventure challenge activities held for her and believed they may be valued by her students as well.	Ms. C. knew that she was an effective teacher and trusted her assessment that infusing self-determination would be positive. She knew part of her effectiveness was due to her positive attitude. To keep her energy high, she needed to take care of her own needs.	Mr. M. believed in his ability as a teacher to assess his students' needs and to develop and implement a curriculum that would be beneficial. He knew he had the right and the responsibility to creatively design instruction that would meet his students' needs.
Plan	Ms. B. planned an experiential activity based on outdoor adventure challenge strategies to augment a specific session in the *Steps to Self-Determination* curriculum. The activity she	Ms. C. developed a plan to implement the *Steps* curriculum that also took into account the amount of time she had available this semester. She adapted some of the sessions to fit within her time	Mr. M. infused the sessions from the *Steps to Self-Determination* curriculum into his creative writing class. He also supplemented the curriculum with several creative writing activities. In addition to the *Steps* activities, he had

(Continued)

Table 9.1 (Continued)

Self-Determination Component	Ms. B. *Special Education Resource Room Teacher*	Ms. C. *Alternative Education Teacher*	Mr. M. *Language Arts Teacher*
	designed asked students to work in teams to devise a way to cross an imaginary river using small pieces of paper as stepping stones. The activity reinforced *Steps* lessons on creativity, taking small steps, and teamwork.	constraints. For example, rather than finding a guest speaker to address the class for Session 11, she asked the students to interview someone about self-determination in their lives.	students write stories about their own daydreams and fictional stories about the dreams of imaginary characters. He began several class sessions with story starters related to self-determination to stimulate student writing.
Act	Ms. B. implemented the lesson and observed responses of the students.	Ms. C. implemented the *Steps* curriculum with the revisions and adaptations she developed. She also continued her regular exercise schedule and got the rest she knew she needed.	Mr. M. implemented the *Steps* sessions and the creative writing adaptations he had designed. He took a risk by trying out several new activities he had not used before.
Experience Outcomes and Learn	Ms. B. was pleased with the student evaluations and made only small alterations to the activity. The activity helped to reinforce the importance of teamwork taught in Session 10 as well as the importance of breaking large goals into small steps in Session 6. She was proud of her accomplishments through this activity.	When Ms. C. reviewed her implementation of the *Steps* curriculum, she was pleased with how the students responded to the adapted activities. However, she decided that if things settled down in the district next year and she had fewer required meetings, she would like to try implementing some of the curriculum activities she had adapted in the way they were recommended in the *Steps* instructor's guide.	Mr. M. asked students to evaluate the class and provide feedback. He found that the focus on self-determination helped to make the creative writing experience personal and meaningful for the students. The creative writing exercises also enhanced the self-determination activities by adding a greater focus on creativity, imagination, and communication skills. He decided he wanted to continue an emphasis on self-determination in creative writing.

Supporting educators to become more self-determined could also have an impact on two major issues currently facing our educational system: stress and retention. To be effective in spite of difficult working conditions, and to change those conditions, teachers need the knowledge, skills, and beliefs of self-determination. Teachers need the ability to prioritize and focus on what is most important in their work. Administrators need strategies to effectively support teachers and advocate for them at an organizational level.

Noddings (1986) eloquently summarized the need for educators to be more self-determined:

> The object of teacher education is not to produce people who will do their duty as it is prescribed or faithfully use the means deemed likely to achieve discrete learning goals but, rather, to produce people who will make autonomous decisions for the sake of their own students. (p. 504)

This statement was echoed by Epanchin, Paul, and Smith (1996): "We want to fortify our graduates [of teacher education programs] with skills and knowledge that enable them to resist and even change school cultures that are coercive, controlling, and unwelcoming to difference" (p. 127). This can only be accomplished if teachers are equipped to teach, and administrators are able to lead, with a sense of self-determination and efficacy.

Interviews with teachers and administrators contributed to our conclusion that self-determination knowledge, skills, and beliefs are as important for teachers as they are for students. A study conducted by Field, Hoffman, and Fullerton (2003) reported the results of interviews with 60 educators who were special education teachers ($n = 25$, 41.7%), general education teachers ($n = 15$, 25%), central office administrators ($n = 10$, 16.7%), or building-level administrators ($n = 10$, 16.7%). Elementary, middle school, and high school teachers were represented in approximately equal proportions. Participants were asked to rate, on a scale of 1 (not important) to 5 (very important), the importance of each of the components of the Field and Hoffman (1994) self-determination model to their work as a teacher or administrator. The question posed to teachers was "To what extent do you believe each of the following knowledge, belief, or skill areas is important to being self-determined as a teacher?"

All 22 self-determination competencies were rated highly by the 60 participants, with a mean response of 4.62 ($SD = .65$) (Figure 9.1). The minimum rating was for "visually rehearse" (3.95), and the maximum rating was for "reflect on and learn from experiences" (4.92) (Table 9.2).

Figure 9.1 Chart of Educators' Ratings of Self-Determination Competencies

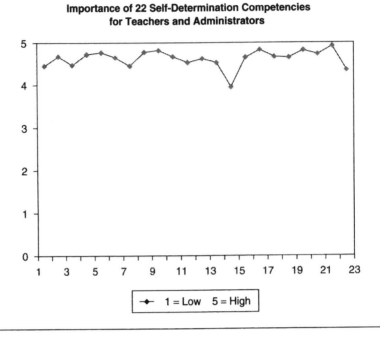

Participants were also asked to provide examples from their careers that demonstrated ways in which the self-determination competencies applied to their work. The 60 educators interviewed provided 246 examples or explanations from their careers as to how self-determination competencies were important for them to be effective on their jobs. The competency for which the most examples were provided was "dream" (8% of all examples). The competency for which the least examples were provided was "reinforce yourself for successes" (2% of all examples). Some examples of the activities offered by the teachers and administrators are provided in Table 9.3.

WHAT DO EDUCATORS NEED TO KNOW TO BE SELF-DETERMINED IN THEIR WORK?

Just as students need to continuously apply knowledge and skills related to self-determination in a variety of settings and learn from their experiences to become increasingly self-determined, so do teachers. Knowledge and skills related to self-determination fluctuate throughout our life span. We may feel very confident in our ability to exercise self-determination in one

Table 9.2 Competency, Mean, and Standard Deviation of Educators' Ratings of Self-Determination Competencies

#	Competency	Mean	SD
1	Dream	4.45	.96
2	Know your strengths, weaknesses, needs, & preferences	4.68	.65
3	Know available options	4.47	.72
4	Know how to make decisions	4.73	.58
5	Accept yourself, with strengths & weaknesses	4.77	.56
6	Accept and address your perceived weaknesses	4.65	.63
7	Know and respect your rights	4.45	.75
8	Know and respect your responsibilities	4.78	.52
9	Take care of yourself	4.82	.39
10	Set goals	4.67	.68
11	Break a goal into small steps	4.53	.83
12	Anticipate potential results of actions	4.62	.64
13	Be creative	4.53	.81
14	Visually rehearse	3.95	1.05
15	Take risks	4.65	.58
16	Clearly communicate	4.83	.56
17	Access resources and support	4.67	.63
18	Negotiate	4.65	.63
19	Deal with conflict and criticism	4.82	.39
20	Be persistent	4.73	.55
21	Reflect on and learn from experiences	4.92	.28
22	Reinforce yourself for successes	4.35	.95

situation and struggle to be self-determined when confronted with new challenges. For example, if you have been teaching in one school for several years with the same preparations and staff, you may feel quite confident in your ability to (a) understand your own strengths and weaknesses related to performing your job, (b) understand the expectations of others around you, (c) set goals that are important to you, and (d) know where you can find support. If you were transferred to a new school, assigned to a different level, and had all new preparations, your ability to exercise self-determination may be diminished. However, your ability to be self-determined would be enhanced by the foundation you built for self-determination in previous settings, and your ability to be self-determined in another new situation would be enhanced by learning to exercise self-determination with another new set of challenges. We learn to be self-determined by acting in a self-determined manner and learning from that

Table 9.3   Educators' Examples of the Need for Self-Determination Competencies

Step/Competency	Example
Step: Know yourself. *Component:* Know your strengths, weaknesses, needs, and preferences.	"For me this year, it took a lot of thought to be able to make the decision to transfer jobs. Knowing where I was stronger as a teacher and what I really preferred, what kind of setting I preferred to be in. I can see where that really has helped me be a better teacher."
Step: Value yourself. *Component:* Take care of yourself.	"I worked with other teachers, and I knew from both my parents being teachers that the work is never done. No matter what you do. I also learned from my parents that doing homework at home during the week is a normal thing to do. I went straight from graduate school to teaching. It's a very natural transition, so managing time wasn't a problem. The time part was easy. I am happily married, and I want to stay that way, and being free on the weekends is part of that for me. . . . The hard part is saying no because everything that people want you to do is wonderful. How can you not support literacy nights or math nights at your school? They buy food, they invite families in, you make games that people can take home and play with their kids. It's a wonderful thing, but I have to say no. I have to do it because I am saying yes to enough things. My plate is full. That's the thing that took me years. It's taken me up to this year to learn, because I used to say yes to everything."
Step: Plan. *Components:* Set goals. Break a goal into small steps.	"There was a principal who came in and there was a meeting going on and they really wanted me to be a part of that meeting, and it was very last minute. So she said, 'I'll take your class so that you can go.' So I gave her the lesson and she changed it and had such wonderful ideas about it. The kids were doing a math lesson integrating language arts. I wanted them to see how many strides it would take to walk around the world. They had to figure out the average stride for their group and then when they did, I just had them use maps and scales and measurements and all of this kind of thing to do the lesson. Well . . . I had never done the lesson before, so in the end, she said, 'You know, I looked at the lesson and I thought no, we can't start there. We really need to start with their desks. How many strides would it take to go on a desk.' Then we talked about the room, then we talked about Michigan, then we talked about the world, which was a hundred times better. It made more sense, but I just felt like I could reflect and deal with that. In a way it was criticism, but it was constructive. And she was just a wonderful lady to work with. So I've learned from that and I break things down now."

Step/Competency	Example
Step: Act. *Component:* Communicate.	"Clearly communicating. I will give you some examples of that. In the South, and it is true today, they use a lot of old English. It has lost its meaning in other places. It doesn't mean exactly what it says somewhere else. For example, the word *directly.* In the South, if my mother called me and I said, 'I will be there directly,' it didn't mean that I was coming immediately. It meant—I'd like to finish what I am doing now and then I am ready to do that. But here, when you say directly, it means immediately. Quite often in the classroom and in talking to people I would have to clarify what it is that I am saying—the meaning behind it. . . . Clearly communicating and speaking in everyday language. When you have rules in your classroom, whatever you stand for, you have to clearly communicate that to students. Once it's clearly communicated, they know that each and every time they see you they have that message."
Step: Experience outcomes and learn.	"I have a little file folder where I put the little thank-you notes that I get from the students that are kind of special or little poems. I stick those in there. I take myself out on Fridays. We go out once in a while just as a staff. It's nice to be able to reward yourself for doing a good job. It is not too often you get praise. The kids don't say it very often. That's why I keep those little letters when I do get them."

experience. We have not met anyone, at any age, who is as self-determined as they would like to be. We have the opportunity to grow in self-determination throughout our life spans.

The model Teaching and Leading With Integrity, Reflection, and Self-Determination (Figure 9.2) illustrates the competencies needed by teachers to apply the concept of self-determination to their work as educators. The model has three basic components:

1. Core knowledge, beliefs, and skills

2. Application of the core knowledge, beliefs, and skills to the educational process

3. Application of the core knowledge, beliefs, and skills across the pre-K through adult continuum

This model is based on the Hoffman and Field (2006) model of self-determination discussed in Chapter 1 and describes the knowledge, beliefs,

Figure 9.2 Teaching and Leading With Integrity, Reflection, and Self-Determination Model

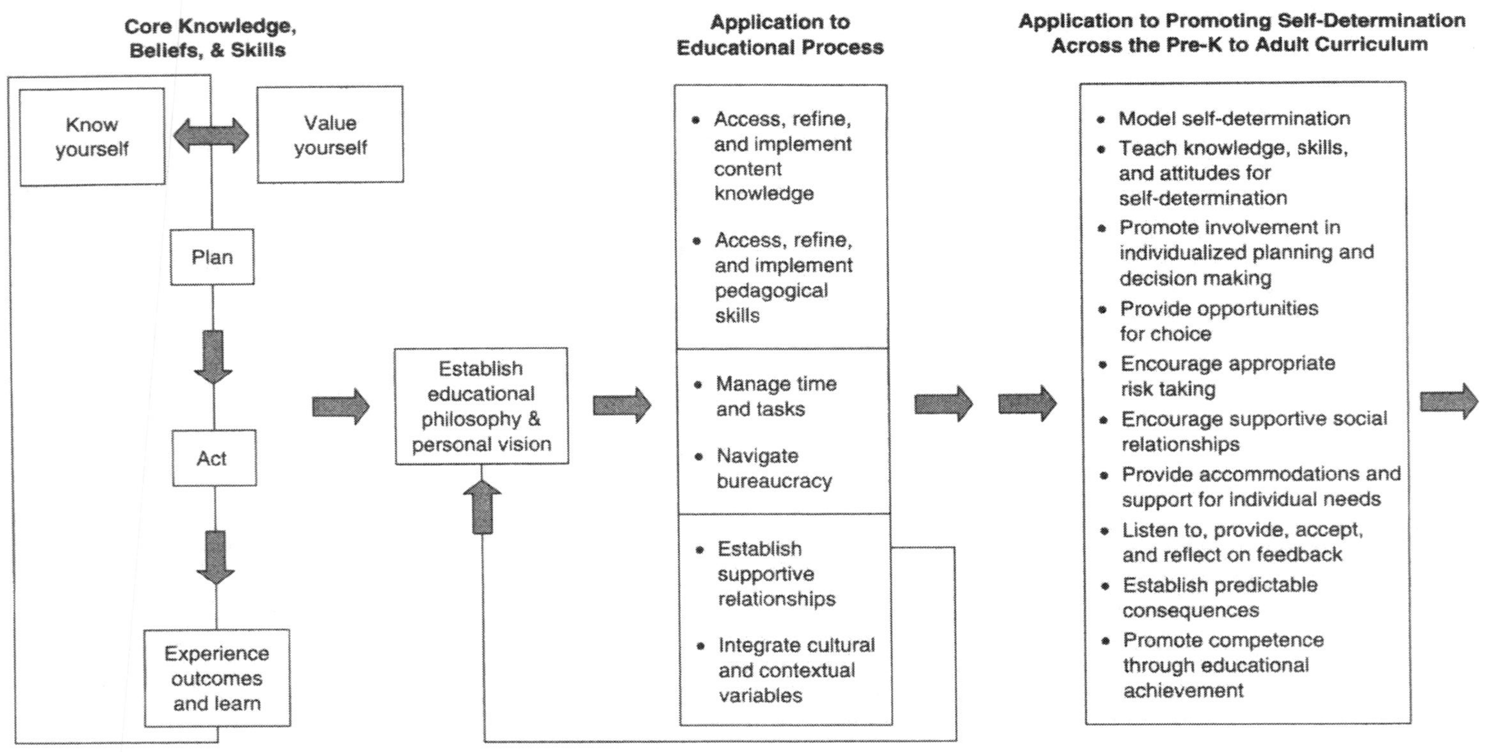

**Core Knowledge,
Beliefs, & Skills**

| Know yourself | Value yourself |

Plan → Act → Experience outcomes and learn

Establish educational philosophy & personal vision

**Application to
Educational Process**

- Access, refine, and implement content knowledge
- Access, refine, and implement pedagogical skills

- Manage time and tasks
- Navigate bureaucracy

- Establish supportive relationships
- Integrate cultural and contextual variables

**Application to Promoting Self-Determination
Across the Pre-K to Adult Curriculum**

- Model self-determination
- Teach knowledge, skills, and attitudes for self-determination
- Promote involvement in individualized planning and decision making
- Provide opportunities for choice
- Encourage appropriate risk taking
- Encourage supportive social relationships
- Provide accommodations and support for individual needs
- Listen to, provide, accept, and reflect on feedback
- Establish predictable consequences
- Promote competence through educational achievement

and skills that help educators increase self-determination within the contexts of their environments. The input from the teacher interviews discussed previously in this chapter was used to develop the model. A national panel comprising teachers, administrators, teacher educators, researchers, and persons with disabilities had input and oversight to the model development.

Seven key themes emerged from interviews conducted with educators about their work (Field et al., 2003). Special attention was given to these themes when delineating how self-determination concepts apply to the work of educators in the Teaching and Leading With Integrity, Reflection, and Self-Determination model. These themes are listed below. Quotes from interviews that illustrate each of the themes are provided.

Having a vision is important to being self-determined in teaching.

"When I think of my legacy . . . I want the school to have a pervasive sense of integrity. This means making decisions that are in the best interests of the children."

"I found a school that has similar goals and philosophies to what I have. I don't think I could work in a place that did not support the beliefs that I have about kids."

Self-reflection and reflective practices promote self-determination.

"As an educator, I believe in reflecting and learning from my experiences because no matter how well any university prepares you, you will have situations that might not be as positive as you thought. The main thing is not to lose the opportunity to learn from them."

"I constantly question myself. I reflect on my practice—who I am and what I would like to be as a person. I think that determines who you are as a leader."

Positive relationships are critical to self-determination.

"I think you have to have a perspective that you are not in this by yourself."

"I am blessed with having a mother who always believed in me."

"A strong support system like my husband and friends. Strong support from administrators and other teachers [helps me be self-determined]."

Bureaucratic and time/task management issues are often seen as challenges to exercising self-determination.

"Dealing with paper [hinders self-determination]."

"Anything to do with the state [hinders self-determination]."

The ability to take care of one's needs supports self-determination.

"It is important to maintain a balance in your life. It's healthy to have things that are totally unrelated to your job . . . otherwise the job will bite you."

"If you don't take care of yourself, no one will. If there is no you, there is nothing."

School structure and environmental issues such as a sense of being valued and opportunities to exercise self-determination are important variables affecting the self-determination of educators.

"When my school principal says, 'you are my most organized teacher,' . . . it makes me feel good. It is the little things that motivate teachers, the little pats on the back. We don't get that very often in our profession."

The ability to focus is a key to being self-determined in teaching.

"You have to set priorities; you have to bring some sense of order to your day. That involves decision making and time management, prioritizing what's most important."

"Anything that is affecting me outside of teaching, I leave outside the door when I walk in. I don't bring it into the classroom."

Through this model, seven key components were identified to apply basic self-determination steps (i.e., know yourself, know your environment, value yourself, plan, act, experience outcomes, and learn) to the responsibilities of teachers and administrators. To exercise increased self-determination in their work, educators need to do the following:

Establish an educational philosophy and vision.

Access, refine, and implement content knowledge.

Access, refine, and implement pedagogical skills.

Manage time and tasks.

Navigate bureaucracy.

Establish supportive relationships.

As you think about the ways in which you do, and don't, engage in your work with a sense of self-determination, you may want to consider the following questions:

Do you have a vision of what you want to accomplish?

Are you enjoying your work?

Do you have mutually supportive relationships with colleagues, supervisors, students, parents, family, and friends?

Have you found ways to stay focused on what you think is most important in your work and to stay away from things that bring you down?

Have you found ways to accomplish the "necessary evils" in your work and minimize the energy taken away from what you think is most important?

Do you have a way of finding some quiet time to reflect and learn from your experiences, to plan and be creative?

Do you take good care of yourself? Do you get enough rest, eat well, exercise, have time with people who are important to you, and do things that you like to do?

WHAT CAN TEACHERS DO TO BUILD AND NURTURE THEIR SELF-DETERMINATION?

Recognition of the importance of self-determination and a commitment to fostering your self-determination are the first steps to becoming more self-determined. As members of one of the helping professions, educators often fall into the trap of putting their total focus on helping others and neglecting to help themselves. As a result, they may find that they end up with less to give to others. Just as the airlines ask adults to put on their own oxygen masks first before they help children put on their masks, the adults in students' lives need to consider their own self-determination as important as that of their students.

Some specific steps you can take to increase your own sense of self-determination are provided below.

1. Learn more about self-determination and how it applies to you. One concrete action you can take to become more self-determined is to learn more about self-determination, and, as you are learning, think about specific ways that you could apply the principles in your life. There are a variety of ways to learn about self-determination. Several resources are provided in the appendix of this book. Some resources that

are specifically geared toward the self-determination of teachers are the *Self-Determination Technical Assistance Resources Start-up (STARS)* CD (Field, 2006) and the *Self-Determined Educator Instructional Modules* (Field et al., 2005).

The *STARS* CD was developed to help transition team members—students and their families, educators, and adult service providers—promote opportunities for students, with or without disabilities, to learn about and exercise self-determination. The CD includes basic information about self-determination, examples of how school districts have infused self-determination instruction and support in their programs, and several tools that educators, families, and agencies can use to begin or expand an emphasis on self-determination instruction. The CD and the accompanying videotape can be used as a self-study tool to learn more about self-determination. You can also use different components of the CD to develop a presentation for others to introduce them to the concept of self-determination. There are sections of the CD that have activities specifically designed for educators to help them increase their own self-determination. In addition, as you explore the CD and learn more about self-determination, you can apply what you're learning to your own role as an educator.

The *Self-Determined Educator Instructional Modules* (Field et al., 2005) were designed to be used in staff development and initial preparation programs to help educators develop self-determination knowledge and skills and apply those skills in a classroom setting. The modules were designed to increase knowledge and skills delineated in the Teaching and Leading With Integrity, Reflection, and Self-Determination model. The modules are experientially based and were designed to be used in a variety of scheduling formats. For example, a module could be used by itself as part of a brown-bag staff development series, three or four modules could be combined to provide a daylong workshop, or many modules could be used over a semester or year as part of a course or as the basis for an ongoing learning community. Some sample modules are described below.

"Is It Me?" by Ann Fullerton, Portland State University, offers a case study of a first-year teacher who is overwhelmed by myriad tasks before her: paperwork, parent requests, and supporting student behavior, to name a few. Participants analyze the case study and are taken through a systematic process where they develop a plan to help her get a handle on the many demands she perceives and to do this in a manner that helps her accomplish what she feels is most important to her in teaching.

"Building Partnerships With Families in Promoting Self-Determination: Respecting Family Diversity" by Ann Turnbull and Mary Morningstar, University of Kansas, helps participants apply the family systems framework in an examination of several family vignettes. The vignettes represent families who have children with disabilities at various age levels and have diverse cultural perspectives related to self-determination.

"Strategies for Using Self-Determination as a Learning Process" by Paula Kohler, Western Michigan University, provides examples and strategies for assignments and activities across the curriculum that include self-determination as a component of the learning process. This module provides a structure for conducting a graduate seminar in a way that also promotes self-determination and self-directed learning. The module includes activities that help participants learn how these strategies could be applied to other instructional content.

In addition to materials developed within the special education field, there are abundant resources related to self-determination in the popular press. A plethora of books, tapes, and CDs focus on components of self-determination such as goal setting and attainment, exercising more control in your life, taking care of yourself, motivation, and well-being. There is so much available that it is often difficult to sift through all of the information to determine what is valuable for you. Some resources we have found in the popular press related to self-determination that we have found to be both substantive and useful include the following:

Finding Your Own North Star by Martha Beck (2001). Beck is a parent of a child with a disability and a frequent columnist for the *Oprah* magazine. She holds a Ph.D. from Harvard and has taught career development at the American Graduate School of International Management. *Finding Your Own North Star* provides resources for readers to identify and act on dreams and desires. The book is witty and enjoyable to read. It includes case studies, questionnaires, and exercises.

What Happy People Know by Dan Baker, Ph.D. (2003). In this book, Baker, a behavioral psychologist and director of the Life Enhancement Program at Canyon Ranch Spa, summarizes scientific research on happiness and provides suggestions for leading a more satisfying life. Many of the traits recent research has indicated are related to happiness are also linked to self-determination. For example, Baker (whose summary of the research on happiness is consistent with several other leading researchers in the field) lists optimism and purpose as qualities that lead to greater happiness. These qualities are also central to self-determination. Baker's book is highly readable, with several stories, interesting anecdotes, and practical suggestions. By focusing on the qualities that will help you find more happiness in your work, you can also increase your self-determination and your effectiveness in your job.

The Inner Game of Work by Timothy Gallwey (2003). Gallwey changed the way we think about coaching and learning in athletics with his popular *Inner Game of Tennis* and *Inner Game of Golf* books. In this book, he applies the same strategies to the work world. His goal is to help readers see the difference between rote performance of a job and rewarding experience in their work. In doing this, he addresses many basic principles of self-determination, including self-awareness, goal setting, taking risks, focusing, and learning from experience. Gallwey stated that his goal in the book is to show readers how to lean how to enjoy doing any job.

2.   Discover your strengths, weaknesses, needs, and preferences on a daily basis. In order to be self-determined, we need to know what is most important to us. We need to understand what our "selves" want and need as well as what we are capable of and what is difficult for us. The best way to learn this is through reflecting on our experiences. A log we have used to help teachers to notice their preferences over a weeklong period is provided in Form 9.1. Teachers have found the log to be useful because it reminds them to notice their own reactions during the day. Also, by recording their likes and dislikes, they are able to review their reactions over a period of time to look for consistencies and differences. We suggest that teachers use this log for a week at a time to give them some insight as to their own preferences related to their jobs.

In addition to the log, an exercise many teachers have found useful to increase their self-awareness is the collage exercise. Gather a variety of magazines, a pair of scissors, a piece of poster board, and some glue sticks. Flip through the magazines and notice things that you like. Don't analyze or give it a lot of thought at this point, just notice what you like, cut it out, and glue it to your board. The amount of time people devote to this activity varies. Some keep cutting out pictures until their board is filled. Others decide that they will work on this activity for about 30 to 45 minutes.

After you have a poster that you are happy with, spend a little time reflecting on it. What do the pictures you chose say about you? Do they give you some insight about what you enjoy and what you value? How can you apply this knowledge to your work as an educator? What could you focus on in your work that will help you target your efforts to your strengths? Many teachers and administrators who have participated in

Form 9.1 Preference Logs

Over the next seven days, keep track of at least three things you enjoy and one thing that you do not enjoy during your day. On days that you are working, focus your list on things that occur related to your work.

Day 1

What I liked	What I disliked
1.	1.
2.	
3.	

Day 2

What I liked	What I disliked
1.	1.
2.	
3.	

Day 3

What I liked	What I disliked
1.	1.
2.	
3.	

(Continued)

Form 9.1 (Continued)

Day 4

What I liked	What I disliked
1.	1.
2.	
3.	

Day 5

What I liked	What I disliked
1.	1.
2.	
3.	

Day 6

What I liked	What I disliked
1.	1.
2.	
3.	

Day 7

What I liked	What I disliked
1.	1.
2.	
3.	

this activity have been surprised by the insights they gained about their preferences and values. This is an activity that can be done as a classroom activity with students, as part of a staff meeting, or on your own.

Another way to increase your understanding of your strengths, weaknesses, needs, and preferences is to try out some new experiences and consider your reactions to them. For example, have you always dreamed of writing a book? Carve a few minutes out of each day and start writing. You may find that you get halfway through the first chapter and it's not your cup of tea. You may find that it's absolutely thrilling. How you will react to taking the action is uncertain. It is more certain that if you reflect on the experience and consider the implications of your reflection for your teaching, you will increase your ability to be more self-determined in your work.

3. Set some goals and move into action. An important component of every instructional effort aimed at self-determination is learning from one's experience. We learn the most about being self-determined by acting in a self-determined manner and reflecting on what happened from that experience. This action and reflection process helps us to determine what we like, what we don't like, and which actions helped us (or didn't help us) achieve our goals. It also helps us sharpen our skills related to self-determination (e.g., decision-making, communication, and interpersonal skills). In many schools, the performance appraisal process offers a chance to determine a goal that is important to you and to work toward it. If you don't have that opportunity in your school, you can decide that you want to set one goal each semester that gives you something important and enjoyable to focus on. When you set a goal, it is important to break the goal down into small steps (just as we encourage students to do), so that the goal can be easily accomplished and that you experience the frequent naturally occurring reinforcement of achievement.

4. Don't go it alone. Find your sources of support. Positive relationships are central to self-determination. Ryan and Deci (2000) identify relationships as one of three pillars of self-determination. Interviews conducted at Wayne State University (e.g., Field et al., 2003) also found that participants placed a high degree of emphasis on the role that positive relationships play in fostering a sense of self-determination. This was particularly evident in interviews conducted with teachers and administrators. When asked "What helps you to be more self-determined?" and "What are the barriers to self-determination?" the answer was often the same—that other people were both the greatest support and the greatest hindrance to self-determination. Relationships are important to self-determination because they provide a secure foundation from which to take risks and try new things. Positive relationships can also provide a sounding board for the process of reflecting on

experiences, a key element of self-determination. Finally, relationships can provide support, both emotional and practical, and often can help us access additional resources.

Self-determination isn't just for students. It's important for teachers and administrators, too. There is nothing selfish about focusing on your own self-determination as part of what you do to be most successful and effective in your work. Many teachers take a colearner approach with their students as they are helping students learn about self-determination. By working on our own self-determination, we are better role models and more effective teachers and leaders for our students.

Resource A

*Self-Determination
Quality Indicators Assessment Tool*

Self-Determination Quality Indicators
Sharon Field, EdD, and Alan Hoffman, EdD
College of Education, Wayne State University

The quality indicators were designed to help school and program teams assess their current self-determination implementation efforts. To inventory present levels of a school or program's performance relative to the self-determination quality indicators, it is recommended that team members identify for each quality indicator ways in which they are meeting the standard as well as areas for improvement. It is also suggested that teams assign a numerical rating for each indicator on a scale of 1 (low) to 4 (high). It may be helpful to have each member of the team rating each of the indicators individually first and then come together as a team to discuss their ratings and arrive at a team consensus rating. Alternatively, teams may choose to assign ratings to each quality indicator through group discussion.

The information from the self-determination self-assessment can be used to set goals for improving the opportunities provided by the program to prepare students in knowledge, beliefs and skills that will help them to be more self-determined. These goals may be at the personal, classroom, school and/or district levels.

To develop a program that is focused on preparing students to be self-determined, it is essential to *act* on the goals developed. Developing and meeting regularly with a supportive team that holds each member accountable for working toward their goals can help assure that goals and plans are turned into action.

The final step in the self-determination process before it re-cycles is "Experience Outcomes and Learn." At a specified point in time, teams need to assess their progress related to promoting student self-determination and celebrate their accomplishments. They also need to determine new goals for their program based on the experience and new knowledge they have developed. It is recommended that program self-assessment be conducted on at least an annual basis after the initial inventory to provide the opportunity for on-going and continuous self-improvement.

School: _____ *General Education:* _____ *Special Education:* _____ *Grade Level:* _____ *District:* _____

Team Members: _____

Quality Indicators	Current Implementation Level		Strengths:
#1:Knowledge, skills, and attitudes for self-determination are addressed in the curriculum, in family support programs and in staff development.	*not implemented*	*fully implemented*	
	DK 1 2	3 4	
1. *Sample Indicators*			
A framework is used to guide systematic infusion of self-determination components in the curriculum. (e.g., Field & Hoffman, 1994; Ward & Kohler, 2001; Wehmeyer, 1996)			**Areas for Growth:**
• *A formal curriculum is used with students to specifically teach knowledge, skills, and beliefs for self-determination.*			
• *Faculty and staff are provided with inservice opportunities to develop self-determination-related skills, such as self-assessment of professional strengths and weaknesses, goal setting, time management.*			
• *Parent-to-parent support groups focused on parent advocacy are available for families.*			

Quality Indicators	Current Implementation Level				Strengths:
#2: Students, parents, and staff are involved participants in individualized educational decision making and planning.	*not implemented* DK	*implemented* 1	2	*fully implemented* 3 4	
1. Sample Indicators					
• *Students and parents are invited to attend I.E.P. meetings and they are encouraged to actively participate in those meetings.*					
• *Students are provided with instruction to help them prepare for active participation in the I.E.P. process.*					**Areas for Growth:**

Quality Indicators	Current Implementation Level					Strengths:
	not implemented DK	1	2	*fully implemented* 3	4	
#3: Students, families, faculty, and staff are provided with opportunities for choice.						
1. *Sample Indicators*						
• *Students participate in their course selection.*						
• *Students can choose from several options as to how they will complete class assignments.*						
• *Families are provided with options about meeting times for conferences.*						
• *Families have meaningful input to the educational decision-making process.*						
• *Faculty and staff are encouraged to express preferences and negotiate regarding teaching assignment and other duties.*						**Areas for Growth:**
• *Faculty participate in the decision-making process related to curriculum standards and selection of curriculum materials.*						

Quality Indicators	Current Implementation Level	Strengths:
#4: Students, families, faculty, and staff are encouraged to take appropriate risks. 1. *Sample Indicators* • *Students are provided with an opportunity to explore coursework and career opportunities that are new to them.* • *Families are encouraged to suggest and experiment with new strategies at home to support the accomplishment of educational objectives.* • *Faculty and staff are encouraged and supported, through the staff development and the supervision/evaluation process, to try new teaching strategies.*	*not implemented* DK 1 2 *fully implemented* 3 4	
		Areas for Growth:

Quality Indicators	Current Implementation Level					Strengths:
#5: Supportive relationships are encouraged.		not implemented DK	1	2	fully implemented 3	4
1. *Sample Indicators*						
• *Peer support programs, such as peer tutoring, peer mentoring, and peer counseling, are provided.*						
• *Students have the opportunity to participate in team projects.*						
• *Families are invited to participate in informal school activities where positive relationships are formed.*						
• *Team teaching is supported.*						
• *Mentoring is provided for new teachers.*						**Areas for Growth:**

Quality Indicators	Current Implementation Level					Strengths:
#6: Accommodations and supports for individual needs are provided.	*not implemented* DK	1	2	*fully implemented* 3	4	
1. *Sample Indicators*						
• *Accommodations necessary for students, family members, and staff with disabilities (e.g., interpreters, modified texts, architectural features) are provided.*						
• *Universal design principles are used in instructional and architectural design.*						**Areas for Growth:**

Quality Indicators	Current Implementation Level					Strengths:
	not implemented DK	1	2	fully implemented 3	4	
#7: Students, families, and staff have the opportunity to express themselves and be understood.						
2. Sample Indicators						
• All students are encouraged to participate in student government activities.						
• Opportunities are provided for dialogue among students and staff during the school day.						
• The expression of divergent opinions by students, families, and staff is encouraged by administrators.						**Areas for Growth:**

Quality Indicators	Current Implementation Level	Strengths:
#8: Consequences for actions are predictable. 3. *Sample Indicators* • *Clearly delineated behavior management plans are available for each classroom.* • *The schoolwide code of conduct for students is explicitly stated.* • *The managerial and decision-making structure of the school is clearly understood by students, families, faculty, and staff.* • *Students can state their goals for educational programs.*	*not implemented* *fully implemented* DK 1 2 3 4	 **Areas for Growth:**

Quality Indicators	Current Implementation Level					Strengths:
#9: Self-determination is modeled throughout the school environment.	*not implemented* DK	*1*	*2*	*3*	*fully implemented* *4*	
4. Sample Indicators						
• *The principal assumes leadership responsibility for conditions within the school.*						
• *Teachers assume leadership responsibility for conditions in their classrooms.*						
• *All school community members (e.g., students, parents, faculty, and staff) are actively involved in the school improvement process.*						**Areas for Growth:**

Resource B

The Arc's Self-Determination Scale

OBTAINING THE ARC'S SELF-DETERMINATION SCALE

Open your Web browser and go to the Beach Center on Disability Web site at http://www.beachcenter.org.

On the home page, click on Books, Manuals and Reports

On the Books, Manuals and Reports page, scroll down to the "View Books and Manuals by General Topic" section and click on the link to Self-Determination.

That will bring up a table of links that include links to the form for The Arc's Self-Determination Scale (in an Adobe Acrobat .pdf format) and The Arc's Self-Determination Scale Procedural Guidelines in a Word document format. The procedural guidelines provide administration, scoring, and psychometric information.

The Arc's Self-Determination Scale is freely available for use but may not be resold or distributed beyond personal use without permission of the authors (wehmeyer@ku.edu). The references for the scale and procedural guidelines are

Wehmeyer, M. L. (1995). *Procedural guidelines for The Arc's Self-Determination Scale*. Arlington, TX: The Arc of the United States.
Wehmeyer, M. L., & Kelchner, K. (1995). *The Arc's Self-Determination Scale*. Arlington, TX: The Arc of the United States.

The Arc's Self-Determination Scale

Adolescent Version

By Michael Wehmeyer, Ph.D.,   Principal Investigator
Kathy Kelchner, M.Ed.,   Project Director
Self-Determination Assessment Project

Student's name _____

Date _____

School _____

Teacher's name _____

The Arc

© 1995

by **The Arc of the United States**

The Arc's Self-Determination Scale (Adolescent Version) is a student self-report measure of self-determination designed for use by adolescents with cognitive disabilities. The scale has two primary purposes:

- To provide students with cognitive disabilities and educators a tool that assists them in identifying student strengths and limitations in the area of self-determination; and
- To provide a research tool to examine the relationship between self-determination and factors that promote/inhibit this important outcome.

The scale has 72 items and is divided into four sections. Each section examines a different essential characteristic of self-determination: Autonomy, Self-Regulation, Psychological Empowerment and Self-Realization. Each section has unique directions that should be read before completing the relevant items. Scoring the scale (see Procedural Guidelines for scoring directions) results in a total self-determination score and subdomain scores in each of the four essential characteristics of self-determination. A comprehensive discussion and exploration of self-determination as an educational outcome is provided in The Arc's Self-Determination Scale Procedural Guidelines, as well as detailed scoring procedures and a discussion about the use of self-report measures in general. The scale **should not be** used until the administrator is thoroughly familiar with these issues.

The Arc's Self-Determination Scale (Adolescent Version) was developed by The Arc National Headquarters with funding from the U. S. Department of Education, Office of Special Education Programs (OSEP), under Cooperative Agreement #H023J20012. Questions used in Section One (Autonomy) were adapted, with permission from the authors, from the Autonomous Functioning Checklist. Questions used in Section 4 (Self-Realization) were adapted, with permission from the author, from the Short form of the Personal Orientation Inventory. Appropriate citations for both instruments are available in The Arc's Self-Determination Scale Procedural Guidelines. The Arc gratefully acknowledges the generosity of these researchers.

Section One
Autonomy

Directions:

Check the answer on each question that BEST tells how you act in that situation. There are no right or wrong answers. Check only one answer for each question. (If your disability limits you from actually performing the activity, but you have control over the activity (such as a personal care attendant), answer like you performed the activity.)

1A. Independence: Routine personal care and family oriented functions

For each item, the response options (checkboxes) are:
I do not even if I have the chance | I do sometimes when I have the chance | I do most of the time I have the chance | I do every time I have the chance

1. I make my own meals or snacks.
2. I care for my own clothes.
3. I do chores in my home.
4. I keep my own personal items together.
5. I do simple first aid or medical care for myself.
6. I keep good personal care and grooming.

1A. Subtotal _____

1B. Independence: Interaction with the environment

7. I make friends with other kids my age.
8. I use the post office.
9. I keep my appointments and meetings.
10. I deal with salespeople at stores and restaurants.

1B. Subtotal _____

1C. Acting on the basis of preferences, beliefs, interests and abilities: Recreational and leisure time

11. I do free time activities based on my interests.
12. I plan weekend activities that I like to do.
13. I am involved in school-related activities.
14. My friends and I choose activities that we want to do.
15. I write letters, notes or talk on the phone to friends and family.
16. I listen to music that I like.

1C. Subtotal _____

1D. Acting on the basis of preferences, beliefs, interests and abilities:
Community involvement and interaction

	I do not even if I have the chance	I do sometimes when I have the chance	I do most of the time I have the chance	I do every time I have the chance
17. I volunteer in things that I am interested in.	☐	☐	☐	☐
18. I go to restaurants that I like.	☐	☐	☐	☐
19. I go to movies, concerts, and dances.	☐	☐	☐	☐
20. I go shopping or spend time at shopping centers or malls.	☐	☐	☐	☐
21. I take part in youth groups (like 4-H, scouting, church groups)	☐	☐	☐	☐

1D. Subtotal _____

1E. Acting on the basis of preferences, beliefs, interests and abilities: Post-school directions

	I do not even if I have the chance	I do sometimes when I have the chance	I do most of the time I have the chance	I do every time I have the chance
22. I do school and free time activities based on my career interests.	☐	☐	☐	☐
23. I work on school work that will improve my career chances.	☐	☐	☐	☐
24. I make long-range career plans.	☐	☐	☐	☐
25. I work or have worked to earn money.	☐	☐	☐	☐
26. I am in or have been in career or job classes or training.	☐	☐	☐	☐
27. I have looked into job interests by visiting work sites or talking to people in that job.	☐	☐	☐	☐

1E. Subtotal _____

1F. Acting on the basis of preferences, beliefs, interests and abilities: Personal expression

	I do not even if I have the chance	I do sometimes when I have the chance	I do most of the time I have the chance	I do every time I have the chance
28. I choose my clothes and the personal items I use every day.	☐	☐	☐	☐
29. I choose my own hair style.	☐	☐	☐	☐
30. I choose gifts to give to family and friends	☐	☐	☐	☐
31. I decorate my own room.	☐	☐	☐	☐
32. I choose how to spend my personal money.	☐	☐	☐	☐

1F. Subtotal _____

Please check Section One, A thru F, to make sure there is only one answer for each question.

Section Two
Self-Regulation

Directions:

Each of the following questions tell the beginning of a story and how the story ends. Your job is to tell what happened in the middle of the story, to connect the beginning and the end. Read the beginning and ending for each question, then fill in the BEST answer for the middle of the story. There are no right or wrong answers.
Remember, fill in the one answer that you think BEST completes the story.

2A. Interpersonal cognitive problem-solving

33. **Beginning:** You are sitting in a planning meeting with your parents and teachers. You want to take a class where you can learn to work as a cashier in a store. Your parents want you to take the Family and Child Care class. You can only take one of the classes.

Middle: _____
_____
_____
_____

Ending: The story ends with you taking a vocational class where you will learn to be a cashier. Story Score _____

34. **Beginning:** You hear a friend talking about a new job opening at the local book store. You love books and want a job. You decide you would like to work at the bookstore.

Middle: _____
_____
_____
_____

Ending: The story ends with you working at the bookstore. Story Score _____

35. **Beginning:** Your friends are acting like they are mad at you. You are upset about this.

Middle: _____
_____
_____
_____

Ending: The story ends with you and your friends getting along just fine. Story Score _____

36. **Beginning:** You go to your English class one morning and discover your English book is not in your backpack. You are upset because you need that book to do your homework.

Middle: _____
_____
_____
_____

Ending: The story ends with you using your English book for homework. Story Score _____

2B: Goal setting and task performance

Directions:

The next three questions ask about your plans for the future. Again, there are no right or wrong answers. For each question, tell if you have made plans for that outcome and, if so, what those plans are and how to meet them.

39. Where do you want to live after you graduate?

☐ I have not planned for that yet.

☐ I want to live _____

List four things you should do to meet this goal:

1) _____
2) _____
3) _____
4) _____

40. Where do you want to work after you graduate?

☐ I have not planned for that yet.

☐ I want to work _____

List four things you should do to meet this goal:

1) _____
2) _____
3) _____
4) _____

41. What type of transportation do you plan to use after graduation?

☐ I have not planned for that yet.

☐ I plan to use _____

List four things you should do to meet this goal:

1) _____
2) _____
3) _____
4) _____

2B Subtotal _____

---

37. **Beginning:** You are in a club at school. The club advisor announces that the club members will need to elect new officers at the next meeting. You want to be the president of the club.

Middle: _____

_____

_____

Story Score _____

Ending: The story ends with you being elected as the club president.

38. **Beginning:** You are at a new school and you don't know anyone. You want to have friends.

Middle: _____

_____

_____

_____

Ending: The story ends with you having many friends at the new school.

Story Score _____

2A Subtotal _____

Section Three

Psychological Empowerment

Directions:

Check the answer that BEST describes you.

Choose only one answer for each question.

There are no right or wrong answers.

42. ☐ I usually do what my friends want... or
    ☐ I tell my friends if they are doing something I don't want to do.

43. ☐ I tell others when I have new or different ideas or opinions... or
    ☐ I usually agree with other peoples' opinions or ideas.

44. ☐ I usually agree with people when they tell me I can't do something... or
    ☐ I tell people when I think I can do something that they tell me I can't.

45. ☐ I tell people when they have hurt my feelings... or
    ☐ I am afraid to tell people when they have hurt my feelings.

46. ☐ I can make my own decisions... or
    ☐ Other people make decisions for me.

47. ☐ Trying hard at school doesn't do me much good... or
    ☐ Trying hard at school will help me get a good job.

48. ☐ I can get what I want by working hard... or
    ☐ I need good luck to get what I want.

49. ☐ It is no use to keep trying because that won't change things... or
    ☐ I keep trying even after I get something wrong.

50. ☐ I have the ability to do the job I want... or
    ☐ I cannot do what it takes to do the job I want.

51. ☐ I don't know how to make friends... or
    ☐ I know how to make friends.

52. ☐ I am able to work with others... or
    ☐ I cannot work well with others.

53. ☐ I do not make good choices... or
    ☐ I can make good choices.

54. ☐ If I have the ability, I will be able to get the job I want... or
    ☐ I probably will not get the job I want even if I have the ability.

55. ☐ I will have a hard time making new friends... or
    ☐ I will be able to make friends in new situations.

56. ☐ I will be able to work with others if I need to... or
    ☐ I will not be able to work with others if I need to.

57. ☐ My choices will not be honored... or
    ☐ I will be able to make choices that are important to me.

Section 3 Subtotal _____

175

Section Four
Self-Realization

#	Statement	Agree	Don't agree
58.	I do not feel ashamed of any of my emotions.	☐	☐
59.	I feel free to be angry at people I care for.	☐	☐
60.	I can show my feelings even when people might see me.	☐	☐
61.	I can like people even if I don't agree with them.	☐	☐
62.	I am afraid of doing things wrong.	☐	☐
63.	It is better to be yourself than to be popular.	☐	☐
64.	I am loved because I give love.	☐	☐
65.	I know what I do best.	☐	☐
66.	I don't accept my own limitations.	☐	☐
67.	I feel I cannot do many things.	☐	☐
68.	I like myself.	☐	☐
69.	I am not an important person.	☐	☐
70.	I know how to make up for my limitations.	☐	☐
71.	Other people like me.	☐	☐
72.	I am confident in my abilities.	☐	☐

Section 4 Subtotal _____

Scoring Step 1:

Record the raw scores from each section:

Autonomy

1A = ☐
1B = ☐
1C = ☐
1D = ☐
1E = ☐
1F = ☐

Domain Total: ☐

Self-Regulation

2A = ☐
2B = ☐

Domain Total: ☐

Psychological Empowerment

3 = ☐

Domain Total: ☐

Self-Realization

4 = ☐

Domain Total: ☐

Scoring Step 3:

Using the conversion tables in Appendix A, convert raw scores into percentile scores for comparison with the sample norms (Norm Sample) and the percentage of positive responses (Positive Scores):

	Norm Sample	Positive Scores

Autonomy

1A = ☐ ☐
1B = ☐ ☐
1C = ☐ ☐
1D = ☐ ☐
1E = ☐ ☐
1F = ☐ ☐
Domain Total: ☐ ☐

Self-Regulation

2A = ☐ ☐
2B = ☐ ☐
Domain Total: ☐ ☐

Psychological Empowerment

3 = ☐ ☐
Domain Total: ☐ ☐

Self-Realization

4 = ☐ ☐
Domain Total: ☐ ☐

Self-Determination Total Score = ☐

Scoring Step 4:

Fill in the graph for the percentile scores from the norming sample. From the appropriate percentile down, darken the complete bar graph (See example in Scoring Manual).

%
100
90
80
70
60
50
40
30
20
10

One A
One B
One C
One D
One E
One F
One
Two A
Two B
Two
Three
Four
Total

Scoring Step 5:

Fill in the graph for the percentile scores indicating the percent positive responses.

%
100
90
80
70
60
50
40
30
20
10

One — Autonomy
Two — Self-Regulation
Three — Psych Empower
Four — Self-Realization
Total — Self-Determination

177

References

Abery, B. H. (1994). A conceptual framework for enhancing self-determination. In M. F. Hayden & B. H. Abery (Eds.), *Challenges for a service system in transition: Ensuring quality community experiences for person with developmental disabilities* (pp. 345–380). Baltimore: Brookes.

Adelman, H. S., & Taylor, L. (1993). *Learning problems and learning disabilities: Moving forward.* Pacific Grove, CA: Brooks/Cole.

Agran, M. (1997). *Student-directed learning: Promoting self-determination.* Pacific Grove, CA: Brooks/Cole.

Agran, M., Blanchard, C., & Wehmeyer, M. L. (2000). Promoting transition goals and self-determination through student self-directed learning: The Self-Determined Learning Model of Instruction. *Education and Training in Mental Retardation and Developmental Disabilities, 35*(4), 351–364.

Agran, M., King-Sears, M., Wehmeyer, M. L., & Copeland, S. R. (2003). *Teachers' guides to inclusive practices: Student-directed learning strategies.* Baltimore: Brookes.

Agran, M., Sinclair, T., Alper, S., Cavin, M., Wehmeyer, M., & Hughes, C. (2005). Using self-monitoring to increase following-direction skills of students with moderate to severe disabilities in general education. *Education and Training in Developmental Disabilities, 40*(1), 3–13.

Algozzine, B., Browder, D., Karvonen, M., Test, D. W., & Wood, W. M. (2001). Effects of intervention to promote self-determination for individuals with disabilities. *Review of Educational Research, 71*, 219–277.

Baker, D. (2003). *What happy people know* (C. Stauth, Illustr.). New York: Rodale.

Bambara, L. M., & Ager, C. (1992). Using self-scheduling to promote self-directed leisure activity in home and community settings. *Journal of the Association for Persons with Severe Handicaps, 17*(2), 67–76.

Bandura, A. (1977). Self-efficacy: Toward a unifying theory of behavioral change. *Psychological Review, 84*(2), 191–215.

Bandura, A. (1986). *Social foundations of thought and action: A social cognitive theory.* Englewood Cliffs, NJ: Prentice Hall.

Bandura, A., & Cervone, D. (2000). Self-evaluative and self-efficacy mechanisms of governing the motivational effects of goal systems. In E. T. Higgins & A. W. Kruglanski (Eds.), *Motivational science: Social and personality perspectives. Key reading in social psychology* (pp. 202–214). Philadelphia: Psychology Press.

Baron, J., & Brown, R. V. (1991). *Teaching decision making to adolescents.* Hillsdale, NJ: Lawrence Erlbaum.

Baumeister, R. F., & Vohs, K. (2004). *Handbook of self-regulation: Research, theory, and applications.* New York: Guilford Press.

Bauminger, N. (2002). The facilitation of social-emotional understanding and social interaction in high-functioning children with autism: Intervention outcomes. *Journal of Autism and Developmental Disorders, 32*(4), 283–298.

Beck, M. (2001). *Finding your own north star: Claiming the life you were meant to live.* New York: Crown.

Bernard-Opitz, V., Sriram, N., & Nakhoda-Sapuan, S. (2001). Enhancing social problem solving in children with autism and normal children through computer-assisted instruction. *Journal of Autism and Developmental Disorders, 31*(4), 377–398.

Beyth-Marom, R., Fischhoff, B., Quadrel, M. J., & Furby, L. (1991). Teaching decision making to adolescents: A critical review. In J. Baron & R. V. Brown (Eds.), *Teaching decision making to adolescents* (pp. 19–59). Hillsdale, NJ: Lawrence Erlbaum.

Biehler, R. F., & Snowman, J. (1993). *Psychology applied to teaching* (7th ed.). Boston: Houghton Mifflin.

Bloom, B. S., Englehart, M. B., Furst, E. J., Hill, W. H., & Krathwohl, D. R. (Eds.). (1956). *Taxonomy of educational objectives. The classification of educational goals. Handbook I: Cognitive domain.* New York: McKay.

Brolin, D. (1997). *Life-centered career education: A life competency approach.* Reston, VA: Council for Exceptional Children.

Brown, F., Appel, C., Corsi, L., & Wenig, B. (1993). Choice diversity for people with severe disabilities. *Education and Training in Mental Retardation, 28*(4), 318–326.

Brown, M. S., Ilderton, P., & Taylor, A. (2001). Twenty ways to include a student with attention problems in the general education classroom. *Intervention in School and Clinic, 37*(1), 50–52.

Byron, J., & Parker, D. R. (2002). College students with ADHD: New challenges and directions. In L. C. Brinckerhoff, J. M. McGuire, & S. F. Shaw (Eds.), *Postsecondary education and transition for students with learning disabilities* (2nd ed., pp. 335–367). Austin, TX: PRO-ED.

Clark, G. M. (1996). Transition planning assessment for secondary-level students with learning disabilities. In J. R. Patton & G. Blalock (Eds.), *Transition and students with learning disabilities: Facilitating the movement from school to adult life* (pp. 131–156). Austin, TX: PRO-ED.

Cooper, K. J., & Browder, D. M. (1998). Enhancing choice and participation for adults with severe disabilities in community-based instruction. *Journal of the Association for Persons with Severe Handicaps, 23,* 252–260.

Coyle, C., & Cole, P. (2004). A videotaped self-modeling and self-monitoring treatment program to decrease off-task behaviour in children with autism. *Journal of Intellectual and Developmental Disabilities, 29*(1), 3–16.

Crone, E. A., Vendel, I., & van der Molen, M. W. (2003). Decision-making in disinhibited adolescents and adults: Insensitivity to future consequences or driven by immediate reward? *Personality and Individual Differences, 35*(7), 1625–1641.

Daly, P. M., & Ranalli, P. (2003). Using countoons to teach self-monitoring skills. *Teaching Exceptional Children, 35*(5), 30–35.

Dattilo, J., & Hoge, G. (1999). Effects of a leisure education program on youth with mental retardation. *Education and Training in Mental Retardation and Developmental Disabilities, 34*(1), 20–34.

Davies, D. M., Stock, S., & Wehmeyer, M. L. (2002). Enhancing independent time management and personal scheduling for individuals with mental retardation through use of a palmtop visual and audio prompting system. *Mental Retardation, 40,* 358–365.

Davis, S., & Wehmeyer, M. L. (1991). *Ten steps to independence: Promoting self-determination in the home.* Arlington, TX: The Arc of the United States.

Deshler, D. D., Ellis, E. S., & Lenz, B. K. (1996). *Teaching adolescents with learning disabilities: Strategies and methods* (2nd ed.). Denver, CO: Love Publishing.

Doll, B., & Sands, D. J. (1998). Student involvement in goals setting and educational decision making: Foundations for effective instruction. In M. L. Wehmeyer & D. J. Sands (Eds.), *Making it happen: Student involvement in education planning, decision making, and instruction* (pp. 45–74). Baltimore: Brookes.

Doll, B., Sands, D. J., Wehmeyer, M. L., & Palmer, S. (1996). Promoting the development and acquisition of self-determined behavior. In D. J. Sands & M. L. Wehmeyer (Eds.), *Self-determination across the life span: Independence and choice for people with disabilities* (pp. 63–88). Baltimore: Brookes.

D'Zurilla, T. J., & Goldfried, M. R. (1971). Problem solving and behavior modification. *Journal of Abnormal Psychology, 78,* 107–126.

D'Zurilla, T. J., & Nezu, A. (1980). A study of the generation-of-alternatives process in social problem solving. *Cognitive Therapy and Research, 4*(1), 67–72.

Eder, R. (1990). Uncovering young children's psychological selves: Individual and developmental differences. *Child Development, 61,* 849–863.

Eisenman, L., & Chamberlin, M. (2001). Implementing self-determination activities: Lessons from schools. *Remedial and Special Education, 22*(3), 138–147.

Epanchin, B. C., Paul, J. L., & Smith, R. L. (1996). The philosophical conundrum of teacher education in special education. *Teacher Education and Special Education, 19*(2), 119–132.

Faherty, C. (2000). *What does it mean to me? A workbook explaining self awareness and life lessons to the child or youth with high functioning autism or Asperger's.* Arlington, TX: Future Horizons.

Fetterman, D. M. (1996). Empowerment evaluation: An introduction to theory and practice. In D. M. Fetterman, S. J. Kaftarian, & A. Wandersman (Eds.), *Empowerment evaluation: Knowledge and tools for self-assessment and accountability* (pp. 3–46). Thousand Oaks, CA: Sage.

Field, S. (1998, April). *Self-determination.* Preconference workshop presented to the Council for Exceptional Children, Minneapolis, MN.

Field, S. (2006). *Self-determination technical assistance resources start-up (STARS)* [CD]. Detroit, MI: Wayne State University, Center for Self-Determination and Transition.

Field, S., & Hoffman, A. (1994). Development of a model for self-determination. *Career Development for Exceptional Individuals, 17*(2), 159–169.

Field, S., & Hoffman, A. (1996). *Steps to self-determination.* Austin, TX: PRO-ED.

Field, S., & Hoffman, A. (2001). *Teaching with integrity, reflection, and self-determination* (Working paper). Detroit, MI: Wayne State University.

Field, S., & Hoffman, A. (2002a, January). Lessons learned from implementing the Steps to Self-Determination curriculum. *Remedial and Special Education, 23*(2), 90–98.

Field, S., & Hoffman, A. (2002b). Preparing youth to exercise self-determination: Quality indicators of school environments that promote the acquisition of knowledge, skills and beliefs related to self-determination. *Journal of Disability Policy Studies, 13*(2), 13–118.

Field, S., Hoffman, A., & Fullerton, A. (2002, April). *Supporting self-determination in the preparation of educators.* Paper presented at the annual meeting of the Council for Exceptional Children, New York.

Field, S., Hoffman, A., & Fullerton, A. (2003). *Self-determination in personnel preparation: Results of a qualitative study* (Working paper). Detroit, MI: Wayne State University.

Field, S., Hoffman, A., & Fullerton, A. (2005). *The self-determined educator: Instructional modules for teacher preparation and development.* Detroit, MI: Wayne State University Press.

Field, S., Hoffman, A., & Les, B. (2006). *Self-determined parenting* (Working paper). Detroit, MI: Wayne State University, Center for Self-Determination and Transition.

Field, S., Hoffman, A., & Sawilowsky, S. (2004). *Self-Determination Assessment Battery.* Detroit, MI: Wayne State University Press.

Field, S., Hoffman, A., Sawilowsky, S., & St. Peter, S. (1996a). *Knowledge and skills for self-determination* (Working paper). Detroit, MI: Wayne State University.

Field, S., Hoffman, A., Sawilowsky, S., & St. Peter, S. (1996b). *Research in self-determination* (Working paper). Detroit, MI: Wayne State University.

Field, S., Martin, J., Miller, R., Ward, M., & Wehmeyer, M. (1998). *A practical guide to teaching self-determination.* Reston, VA: Council for Exceptional Children.

Frea, W. D., Arnold, C. L., & Vittimberga, G. L. (2001). A demonstration of the effects of augmentative communication on the extreme aggressive behavior of a child with autism within an integrated preschool setting. *Journal of Positive Behavior Interventions, 3*(4), 194–198.

Fullan, M., & Miles, M. (1992). Getting reform right: What works and what doesn't. *Phi Delta Kappan, 73*(10), 744–752.

Furby, L., & Beyth-Marom, R. (1992). Risk taking in adolescence: A decision-making perspective. *Developmental Review, 12*(1), 1–44.

Gallwey, W. T. (2000). *The inner game of work.* New York: Random House.

Gilberts, G. H., Agran, M., Hughes, C., & Wehmeyer, M. (2001). The effects of peer-delivered self-monitoring strategies on the participation of students with severe disabilities in general education classrooms. *Journal of the Association for Persons with Severe Handicaps, 26*(1), 25–36.

Gordon, R. L. (1977). *Unidimensional scaling of social variables: Concepts and procedures.* New York: Free Press.

Graham, S., & Harris, K. (2005). *Writing better: Effective strategies for teaching students with learning difficulties.* Baltimore: Brookes.

Guerra, N. G., Moore, A., & Slaby, R. G. (1995). *Viewpoints: A guide to conflict resolution and decision making for adolescents.* Champaign, IL: Research Press.

Gumpel, T. P., Tappe, P., & Araki, C. (2000). Comparison of social problem-solving abilities among adults with and without developmental disabilities. *Education and Training in Mental Retardation and Developmental Disabilities, 35*, 259–268.

Hagborg, W. J. (1996). Self-concept and middle school students with learning disabilities: A comparison of scholastic competence subgroups. *Learning Disability Quarterly, 19*(2), 117–126.

Halpern, A. S., Herr, C. M., Doren, B., & Wolf, N. K. (2000). *NEXT S.T.E.P.: Student transition and educational planning* (2nd ed.). Austin, TX: PRO-ED.

Haring, N. G., Liberty, K. A., & White, O. R. (1980). Rules for data-based strategy decisions in instructional programs: Current research and instructional implications. In W. Sailor, B. Wilcox, & L. Brown (Eds.), *Methods of instruction for severely handicapped students* (pp. 159–192). Baltimore: Brookes.

Harris, K. R., Friedlander, B. D., Saddler, B., Frizzelle, R., & Graham, S. (2005). Self-monitoring of attention versus self-monitoring of academic performance. *Journal of Special Education, 39*(3), 145–156.

Hoffman, A., & Field, S. (2006). *Steps to self-determination* (2nd ed.). Austin, TX: PRO-ED.

Hogarth, R. M. (1980). *Judgement and choice: The psychology of decision.* New York: Wiley.

Hughes, C., & Agran, M. (1993). Teaching persons with severe disabilities to use self-instruction in community settings: An analysis of applications. *Journal of the Association for Persons with Severe Handicaps, 18*, 261–274.

Hughes, C., Copeland, S. R., Agran, M., Wehmeyer, M. L., Rodi, M. S., & Presley, J. A. (2002). Using self-monitoring to improve performance in general education high school classes. *Education and Training in Mental Retardation and Developmental Disabilities, 37*(3), 262–271.

Izzo, M. V., Pritz, S. G., & Ott, P. (1990). Teaching problem-solving skills: A ticket to a brighter future. *Journal for Vocational Special Needs Education, 13*, 23–26.

Jacobs, H. H. (1997). *Mapping the big picture: Integrating curriculum and assessment K–12.* Washington, DC: Association for Supervision and Curriculum Development.

Janis, I., & Mann, L. (1977). *Decision making: A psychological analysis of conflict, choice and commitment.* New York: Free Press.

Janney, R., & Snell, M. (2000). *Teachers' guides to inclusive practices: Modifying schoolwork.* Baltimore: Brookes.

Jitendra, A. K., Hoppes, M. K., & Zin, Y. P. (2000). Enhancing main idea comprehension for students with learning problems: The role of summarization strategy and self-monitoring instruction. *Journal of Special Education, 34*(3), 127–139.

Johnson, D., Johnson, R., Holubec, E., & Roy, P. (1984). *Circles of learning.* Alexandria, VA: Association for Supervision and Curriculum Development.

Johnson, D. L., & Johnson, R. (1986). Mainstreaming and cooperative learning strategies. *Exceptional Children, 52*(6), 553–561.

Johnson, D. W., Johnson, R. T., & Maruyama, G. (1983). Interdependence and interpersonal attraction among heterogeneous and homogeneous individuals: A theoretical formulation and a meta-analysis of the research. *Review of Educational Research, 53*, 5–54.

Joyce, B., & Weil, M. (1980). *Models of teaching* (2nd ed.). Englewood Cliffs, NJ: Prentice Hall.

Kalyanpur, M., & Harry, B. (1999). *Culture in special education: Building reciprocal family-professional relationships.* Baltimore: Brookes.

Kame'enui, E. J., & Simmons, D. C. (1999). *Toward successful inclusion of students with disabilities: The architecture of instruction.* Arlington, VA: Council for Exceptional Children.

Karvonen, M., Test, D. W., Wood, W. M., Browder, D., & Algozzine, B. (2004). Putting self-determination into practice. *Exceptional Children, 71*(1), 23–41.

Khemka, I. (2000). Increasing independent decision-making skills of women with mental retardation in simulated interpersonal situations of abuse. *American Journal on Mental Retardation, 105*(5), 387–401.

Knowlton, E. (1998). Considerations in the design of personalized curricular supports for students with developmental disabilities. *Education and Training in Mental Retardation and Developmental Disabilities, 33*(2), 95–107.

Kochhar-Bryant, C., & Bassett, D. (2003). *Aligning transition and standards-based education: Issues and strategies.* Arlington, VA: Council for Exceptional Children.

Koestner, R., Ryan, R. M., Bernieri, R., & Holt, K. (1984). The effects of controlling versus information limit-setting styles on children's intrinsic motivation and creativity. *Journal of Personality, 52*, 233–248.

Kohler, P. D., & Ward, M. J. (2001). *Planning guide for integrating self-determination skills and application across the curriculum.* Kalamazoo: Western Michigan University.

Latham, G. P., & Locke, E. A. (1991). Self-regulation through goal setting. *Organizational Behavior and Human Decision Processes, 50*(2), 212–247.

Lehmann, J. (1993). *Sharing the journey.* Unpublished manuscript, Colorado State University, Fort Collins.

Levendoski, L. S., & Cartledge, G. (2000). Self-monitoring for elementary school children with serious emotional disturbances: Classroom applications for increased academic responding. *Behavioral Disorders, 25*(3), 211–224.

Locke, E. A., & Latham, G. P. (1990). *A theory of goal setting & task performance.* Upper Saddle River, NJ: Prentice Hall.

Lovitt, T. C. (1989). *Introduction to learning disabilities.* Boston: Allyn & Bacon.

Martin, J. (1997, October). *Self-determination is for teachers too.* Presentation to the Division on Career Development and Transition International Conference, Scottsdale, AZ.

Martin, J. E., & Marshall, L. H. (1995). *ChoiceMaker Self-Determination instructional package.* Longmont, CO: Sopris West.

Martin, J. E., Marshall, L., Maxson, L. L., & Jerman, P. (1993). *Self-directed IEP.* Longmont, CO: Sopris West.

McGahee-Kovac, M. (2002). *A student's guide to the IEP.* Washington, DC: National Information Center for Children and Youth with Disabilities.

McTighe, J., Seif, E., & Wiggins, G. (2004). You can teach for meaning. *Educational Leadership, 62*(1), 26.

Meichenbaum, D., & Biemiller, A. (1998). *Nurturing independent learners: Helping students take charge of their learning.* Cambridge, MA: Brookline Books.

Meichenbaum, D., & Goodman, J. (1971). Training impulsive children to talk to themselves: A means of developing self-control. *Journal of Abnormal Psychology, 77*(2), 115–126.

Mithaug, D. E. (1993). *Self-regulation theory: How optimal adjustment maximizes gain.* Westport, CT: Praeger/Greenwood.

Mithaug, D. E., Mithaug, D. K., Agran, M., Martin, J. E., & Wehmeyer, M. L. (Eds.). (2003). *Self-determined learning theory: Construction, verification, and evaluation.* Mahwah, NJ: Lawrence Erlbaum.

Moore, K. D. (2005). *Effective instructional strategies: From theory to practice.* Thousand Oaks, CA: Sage.

National Information Center for Children and Youth With Disabilities. (2002). *Helping students develop their IEPs* (2nd ed.). Washington, DC: Author.

Noddings, N. (1986). Fidelity in teaching, teacher education, and research for teaching. *Harvard Educational Review, 56*(4), 496–510.

Nolet, V., & McLaughlin, M. (2000). *Accessing the general curriculum.* Thousand Oaks, CA: Corwin Press.

O'Reilly, M. F., Lancioni, G. E., & O'Kane, N. (2000). Using a problem solving approach to teach social skills to workers with brain injuries in supported employment settings. *Journal of Vocational Rehabilitation, 14*(3), 187–194.

Orkwis, R., & McLane, K. (1998, Fall). *A curriculum every student can use: Design principles for student access* (ERIC/OSEP Topical Brief). Reston, VA: Council for Exceptional Children.

Palmer, S., & Wehmeyer, M. L. (2002). *Self-determined learning model for early elementary students: A parent's guide.* Lawrence, KS: University of Kansas, Beach Center on Disability, Schiefelbusch Institute for Lifespan Studies.

Palmer, S. B., Wehmeyer, M. L., Gibson, K., & Agran, M. (2004). Promoting access to the general curriculum by teaching self-determination skills. *Exceptional Children, 70*(4), 427–439.

Parker, D., & Byron, J. (1998). Differences between college students with LD and AD/HD: Practical implications for service providers. In P. Quinn & A. McCormick (Eds.), *Re-thinking AD/HD: A guide to fostering success in students with AD/HD at the college level* (pp. 14–30). Bethesda, MD: Advantage Books.

Powers, L. (1997). *Self-determination is for teachers too.* Presentation to the Division on Career Development International Conference, Scottsdale, AZ.

Powers, L. E., Ellison, R., Matuszewski, J., & Turner, A. (2004). *TAKE CHARGE for the future.* Portland, OR: Portland State University Regional Resource Center.

Pressley, M. (2005). *Reading instruction that works: The case for balanced teaching* (3rd ed.). New York: Guilford Press.

Reid, R. (1996). Research in self-monitoring with students with disabilities: The present, the prospects, and the pitfalls. *Journal of Learning Disabilities, 29*(3), 317–331.

Reinhartsen, D. B., Garfinkle, A. N., & Wolery, M. (2002). Engagement with toys in two-year-old children with autism: Teacher selection versus child choice. *Research and Practice for Persons with Severe Disabilities, 27*(3), 175–187.

Riffel, L. A., Wehmeyer, M. L., Turnbull, A. P., Lattimore, J., Davies, D., Stock, S., et al. (2005). Promoting independent performance of transition-related tasks using a palmtop PC-based self-directed visual and auditory prompting system. *Journal of Special Education Technology, 20*(2), 5–14.

Rose, D., & Meyer, A. (2002). *Teaching every student in the digital age: Universal design for learning.* Alexandria, VA: Association for Supervision and Curriculum Development.

Rotter, J. B. (1954). *Social learning and clinical psychology.* Englewood Cliffs, NJ: Prentice Hall.

Rotter, J. B. (1966). Generalized expectancies for internal versus external control of reinforcement. *Psychological Monographs, 80*(1), 244–248.

Ryan, R. M., & Deci, E. L. (2000). Self-determination theory and the facilitation of intrinsic motivation, social development, and well-being. *American Psychologist, 55*(1), 68–78.

Sarver, M. D. (2000). *A study of the relationship between personal and environmental factors bearing on self-determination and the academic success of university students with learning disabilities.* Unpublished doctoral dissertation, University of Florida, Gainesville.

Schalock, R. L. (1996). Reconsidering the conceptualization and measurement of quality of life. In R. Schalock (Ed.), *Quality of life: Conceptualization and measurement* (Vol. 1, pp. 123–139). Washington, DC: American Association on Mental Retardation.

Schloss, P. J., & Smith, M. A. (1998). *Applied behavior analysis in the classroom* (2nd ed.). Boston: Allyn & Bacon.

Schunk, D. H., & Zimmerman, B. J. (1998). *Self-regulated learning: From teaching to self-reflective practice.* New York: Guilford Press.

Seligman, M. (1995). *The optimistic child.* New York: Houghton Mifflin.

Serna, L. A., Nielsen, E., & Forness, S. R. (in press). *Social stories and songs for children.* Champaign, IL: Research Press.

Shogren, K. A., Faggella-Luby, M., Bae, S. J., & Wehmeyer, M. L. (2004). The effect of choice-making as an intervention for problem behavior: A meta-analysis. *Journal of Positive Behavior Interventions, 6*(4), 228–237.

Smith, D. D. (1989). *Teaching students with learning and behavior problems* (2nd ed.). Englewood Cliffs, NJ: Prentice Hall.

Sorenson, J. S., Buckmaster, L. R., Francis, M. K., & Knauf, K. M. (1996). *The power of problem solving: Practical ides and teaching strategies for any K-8 subject area.* Boston: Allyn & Bacon.

Sowers, J., & Powers, L. (1995). Enhancing the participation and independence of students with severe physical and multiple disabilities in performing community activities. *Mental Retardation, 33*(4), 209–220.

Storey, K. (2002). Strategies for increasing interactions in supported employment settings: An updated review. *Journal of Vocational Rehabilitation, 17*(4), 231–237.

Turnbull, A. P., & Turnbull, H. R. (1996). Self-determination within a culturally responsive family systems perspective. In L. E. Powers, G. H. S. Singer, & J. Sowers (Eds.), *On the road to autonomy: Promoting self-determination in children and youth with disabilities* (pp. 195–220). Baltimore: Brookes.

Turnbull, A. P., & Turnbull, H. R. (2001). *Families, professionals, and exceptionality: Collaborating for empowerment* (4th ed.). Upper Saddle River, NJ: Merrill/Prentice Hall.

Turnbull, H. R., Turnbull, A. P., & Wehmeyer, M. L. (2006). *Exceptional lives: Special education in today's schools* (5th ed.). Upper Saddle River, NJ: Merrill/Prentice Hall.

Turnbull, H. R., Turnbull, A. P., Wehmeyer, M. L., & Park, J. (2003). A quality of life framework for special education outcomes. *Remedial and Special Education, 24*(2), 67–74.

Uberti, H. Z., Mastopieri, M., & Scruggs, T. (2004). Check it off: Individualizing a math algorithm for students with disabilities via self-monitoring checklist. *Intervention in School and Clinic, 39*(5), 269–275.

Van Reusen, A. K., Bos, C. S., Schumaker, J. B., & Deshler, D. D. (2002). *The self-advocacy strategy for enhancing student motivation and self-determination.* Lawrence, KS: Edge Enterprises.

Wall, M., & Dattilo, J. (1995). Creating option-rich learning environments: Facilitating self-determination. *Journal of Special Education, 29*(3), 276–294.

Ward, M. J., & Meyer, R. N. (1999). Self-determination for people with developmental disabilities and autism: Two self-advocates' perspectives. *Focus on Autism and Other Developmental Disabilities, 14*(3), 133–139.

Watanabe, M., & Sturmey, P. (2003). The effect of choice-making opportunities during activity schedules on task engagement of adults with autism. *Journal of Autism and Developmental Disorders, 33*(5), 535–538.

Wehmeyer, M. L. (1992). Self-determination and the education of students with mental retardation. *Education and Training in Mental Retardation, 27,* 302–314.

Wehmeyer, M. L. (1994). Employment status and perceptions of control of adults with cognitive and developmental disabilities. *Research in Developmental Disabilities, 15*(2), 119–131.

Wehmeyer, M. L. (1995). A career education approach: Self-determination for youth with mild cognitive disabilities. *Intervention in School and Clinic, 30*(3), 157–163.

Wehmeyer, M. L. (1996). Self-determination as an educational outcome: How does it relate to the educational needs of our children and youth? In D. J. Sands & M. L. Wehmeyer (Eds.), *Self-determination across the life span: Independence and choice for people with disabilities* (pp. 17–36). Baltimore: Brookes.

Wehmeyer, M. L. (1999). A functional model of self-determination: Describing development and implementing instruction. *Focus on Autism and Other Developmental Disabilities, 14*(1), 53–61.

Wehmeyer, M. L. (2000). *Access to the general curriculum for high school students with mental retardation: Curriculum adaptation, augmentation and alteration.* Unpublished grant proposal.

Wehmeyer, M. L. (2001). Self-determination and mental retardation. In L. M. Glidden (Ed.), *International review of research in mental retardation* (Vol. 24, pp. 1–48). San Diego, CA: Academic Press.

Wehmeyer, M. L. (2006). Self-determination and individuals with severe disabilities: Reexamining meanings and misinterpretations. *Research and Practice in Severe Disabilities, 30,* 113–120.

Wehmeyer, M. L., Abery, B., Mithaug, D. E., & Stancliffe, R. J. (2003). *Theory in self-determination: Foundations for educational practice.* Springfield, IL: Charles C Thomas.

Wehmeyer, M. L., Agran, M., & Hughes, C. (1998). *Teaching self-determination to students with disabilities: Basic skills for successful transition.* Baltimore: Brookes.

Wehmeyer, M. L., & Bolding, N. (1999). Self-determination across living and working environments: A matched-samples study of adults with mental retardation. *Mental Retardation, 37*(5), 353–363.

Wehmeyer, M. L., & Bolding, N. (2001). Enhanced self-determination of adults with mental retardation as an outcome of moving to community-based work or living environments. *Journal of Intellectual Disability Research, 45*(5), 371–383.

Wehmeyer, M. L., & Kelchner, K. (1995). *The Arc's Self-Determination Scale.* Arlington, TX: The Arc of the United States.

Wehmeyer, M. L., Lattin, D., & Agran, M. (2001). Promoting access to the general curriculum for students with mental retardation: A decision-making model. *Education and Training in Mental Retardation and Developmental Disabilities, 36*(4), 329–344.

Wehmeyer, M. L., & Lawrence, M. (1995). Whose future is it anyway? Promoting student involvement in transition planning. *Career Development for Exceptional Individuals, 18*(1), 69–83.

Wehmeyer, M. L., Lawrence, M., Kelchner, K., Palmer, S., Garner, N., & Soukup, J. (2004). *Whose future is it anyway? A student-directed transition planning process* (2nd ed.). Lawrence, KS: Beach Center on Disability.

Wehmeyer, M. L., & Palmer, S. (2003). Adult outcomes for students with cognitive disabilities three years after high school: The impact of self-determination. *Education and Training in Developmental Disabilities, 38*(2), 131–144.

Wehmeyer, M. L., Palmer, S. B., Agran, M., Mithaug, D. E., & Martin, J. E. (2000). Promoting causal agency: The self-determined learning model of instruction. *Exceptional Children, 66*(4), 439–453.

Wehmeyer, M. L., Sands, D. J., Doll, B., & Palmer, S. B. (1997). The development of self-determination and implications for educational interventions with students with disabilities. *International Journal of Disability, Development, and Education, 44*(4), 212–225.

Wehmeyer, M. L., Sands, D. J., Knowlton, E. H., & Kozleski, E. (2002). *Teaching students with mental retardation: Promoting access to the general curriculum.* Baltimore: Brookes.

Wehmeyer, M. L., & Schwartz, M. (1997). Self-determination and positive adult outcomes: A follow-up study of youth with mental retardation or learning disabilities. *Exceptional Children, 63*(2), 245–255.

Wehmeyer, M. L., & Schwartz, M. (1998). The relationship between self-determination and quality of life for adults with mental retardation. *Education and Training in Mental Retardation and Developmental Disabilities, 33*(1), 3–12.

Whitman, T. L. (1990). Self-regulation and mental retardation. *American Journal on Mental Retardation, 94,* 347–362.

Wiener, J. (2004). Do peer relationships foster behavioral adjustment in children with learning disabilities? *Learning Disabilities Quarterly, 27*(1), 21–30.

Wiggins, G., & McTighe, J. (1998). *Understanding by design.* Alexandria, VA: Association for Supervision and Curriculum Development.

Wolman, J. M., Campeau, P. L., Dubois, P. A., Mithaug, D. E., & Stolarski, V. S. (1994). *AIR Self-Determination Scale and user guide.* Palo Alto, CA: American Institutes for Research.

Zimmerman, M. A. (1990). Toward a theory of learned hopefulness: A structural model analysis of participation and empowerment. *Journal of Research in Personality, 24,* 71–86.

Index

CORWIN PRESS

The Corwin Press logo—a raven striding across an open book—represents the union of courage and learning. Corwin Press is committed to improving education for all learners by publishing books and other professional development resources for those serving the field of PreK–12 education. By providing practical, hands-on materials, Corwin Press continues to carry out the promise of its motto: **"Helping Educators Do Their Work Better."**

17463057R00111

Made in the USA
Lexington, KY
11 September 2012